P9-BIF-613

A13mw #18-

Standard Encyclopedia of

Millersburg Crystal

Identification and Values

Bill Edwards
& Mike Carwile

COLLECTOR BOOKS
A Division of Schroeder Publishing Co., Inc.

The current values in this book should be used only as a guide. They are not intended to set prices, which vary from one section of the country to another. Auction prices as well as dealer prices vary greatly and are affected by condition as well as demand. Neither the authors nor the publisher assumes responsibility for any losses that might be incurred as a result of consulting this guide.

Front Cover:

Top right: Hobstar & Feather covered butter dish
Lower right: Ohio Star cider pitcher
Lower left: Hobstar & Feather spittoon whimsey

Back Cover:

Top: Hobstar & Feather large rose bowl (frosted)
Middle: Potpourri milk pitcher
Bottom: Flute (Peacock blank) compote with clover base

Cover design by Terri Hunter
Book design by Sherry Kraus

Searching For A Publisher?

We are always looking for people knowledgeable within their fields. If you feel that there is a real need for a book on your collectible subject and have a large comprehensive collection, contact Collector Books.

Collector Books
P.O. Box 3009
Paducah, Kentucky 42002-3009

www.collectorbooks.com

Copyright © 2001 by Bill Edwards & Mike Carwile

All rights reserved. No part of this book may be reproduced, stored in any retrieval system, or transmitted in any form, or by any means including but not limited to electronic, mechanical, photocopying, recording, or otherwise, without the written consent of the authors and publisher.

Contents

Dedication

To the people of Millersburg who have kept the dream alive by recognizing the blessings they were given.

Acknowledgments

We want to extend our thanks to the following people who have contributed to the publication of this book in one way or another. Many shared photos, others gave us information or Millersburg mementos. A special thanks to all of you: Larry Cullen, Ben Hershberger, John and Rayann Calai, Mr. And Mrs. Norman Archer, Steve Magg, Rick and Bonnie Boldt, Harold Smith, Sherry Smith, Randall Cullen (12 years old and already a Millersburg collector), Frank M. Fenton and the staff of the Fenton Art Glass Company museum, Howard Seufer for photographing glass at Fenton, Wally McDaniel, Richard and Merri Houghton, Mr. and Mrs. Russell Bibbee, Sonny Hall, Gene Mizer, Wes Schmucker, Mike Young, Don Doyle, the Elliott Sheelys, Gary, Eve, and Michael Lickver, Mark Boley, Terry Hall, Steve Hall, Harold Wagner, the Marion Westons, and anyone else we may have unintentionally overlooked. Bless all of you!

The authors can be contacted at:

Bill Edwards
620 W. 2nd St.
Madison, IN 47250
(812) 265-2940

Mike Carwile
180 Cheyenne Dr.
Lynchburg, VA 24502
(434) 237-4247
carwile@centralva.net

Author's Note

When I wrote the first book about Millersburg crystal, I did a bit of speculating about two patterns which many of us at that time felt might be from the Millersburg Company. But like most things, time has cleared away the possibilities and we now know neither of these patterns was from Millersburg. I refer to Palm Wreath (aka: Fernburst) which was advertised in a Westmoreland ad before the Millersburg factory existed, and the Hobstar Fancy which appeared in ads in 1907, also before the Millersburg plant produced glass.

In addition, I showed what we thought at the time were pieces of Millersburg Diamonds in crystal and ruby stain, but since then they have proven to be the similar Manhattan pattern by Tarentum Glass Company of Tarentum, Pennsylvania. But do not think Millersburg Diamonds doesn't exist in crystal, for it certainly does, and pieces are shown in this book. We know the punch set as well as the water set were in crystal production and examples of the punch base, a tumbler, and pitcher are known. In addition, a tumbler in amethyst is shown.

Tarentum's Manhattan was made in a vinegar cruet, syrup, salt shaker, stemmed cake salver, and a compote as well as a goblet. None of these shapes were made in Diamonds but the punch stand (or base) has been seen whimsied into a compote shape.

We hope this brief overview will be helpful to future collectors and will stop the sales of patterns that were attributed to Millersburg in the past, but are known now as someone else's glass, at Millersburg prices.

Introduction

In 1981, I wrote a small book, printed in black and white, called *Millersburg Crystal*. It was a follow-up book to my *Millersburg, Queen of Carnival Glass*, and was intended to complete the Millersburg story. Both books sold well (the carnival book was in print for seven years) and both still sell today on the secondary book market, but in fact neither of them finished the story I had set out to tell, because we are always learning new things about this remarkable company and its glass.

Time went by and I got caught up in other book projects but I never stopped wanting to return to the topic of Millersburg, especially their crystal, and give it a larger look. In 1997 I started my second collection of this glass and knew it was my first love in collecting. Millersburg crystal was becoming "hot" again and I wished we could add all the never-before-reported shapes and treatments we were finding. When my co-author and I discussed a new crystal book, I was enthusiastic but didn't get my hopes up, despite being urged to do a crystal book by many collectors at the 1999 Millersburg Fall Festival. In early January of this year, Mike and I talked about it again, and a few days later, our editor, Lisa Stroup, told me she had talked to Bill (Schroeder) about such a book, and he said "go for it!"

So now, after two decades, we are returning to the scene of this wonderful glass and I couldn't be happier. We hope all those who collect Millersburg crystal will be just as excited as we are, and especially those in the town of Millersburg and in Holmes County, who have made it such an important glass in the collecting world today. (As is said in the trades, Millersburg crystal is a "hot ticket" today, and even badly damaged items sell for premium prices on eBay, Yahoo, or Amazon.com.)

We've tried in this upgraded book to bring some fresh information to the table and to add as much insight to the mix as we've been able to learn over the past two decades. Certainly, working on this project has been one of the best experiences of my life, like visiting with an old friend, and we only hope readers will have as pleasant an experience as we've had.

Bill Edwards

Millersburg Story

In 1903, John and Frank Fenton came to Martins Ferry, Ohio, to begin a glass business after working for several other glass firms. Both worked at Northwood as did Charles H. Fenton, another brother, who later joined John and Frank at the decorating plant.

John W. Fenton and Frank L. Fenton were almost opposites in personality. Frank was quiet, conservative, and level-headed; John, eleven years older, was eager, brash, and a dreamer, often recognized as the family's pitchman. Frank apprenticed at Indiana Glass, becoming foreman in 1898, and in 1900 had gone to Jefferson Glass, then Bastow Glass, and finally to Northwood. John had mentioned at a family gathering that if Frank ever wanted to go into the glass business with him, to let him know. In 1903 they came to Martins Ferry. The Fenton Art Glass Company began with J.C. Dent as president, a druggist who had put up substantial funds for stock. The treasurer was a Dr. Howells who had also helped with funds.

Fenton Art Glass began as a glass decorating shop in an abandoned factory they had rented, buying other companies' blanks and cutting designs for resale. When finances grew, land was purchased in Williamstown, West Virginia, subdivided into lots, and sold for additional cash, and finally factory construction was begun.

By 1907 the Fenton factory was a going concern and a recognized producer of iridized glass, using a process they developed. In early 1908, the partnership had begun to fray because of the diverse personalities of John and Frank L., with John finally deciding to move on. He soon severed his ties and relinquished his brief presidency (he was elected president after moving to Williamstown in November 1907, when Dent and J.O. Howells had resigned their positions to become directors). John was 38 years old, a huge, strapping man with a shock of brown hair, a strong mustache, and steely eyes that could almost hypnotize. He would sire five children and outlive all but two.

After weeks of inquiry, John came to Holmes County, Ohio, and was instantly impressed with the countryside and the work ethic of the people. Word soon spread that he felt Millersburg was a good place for a glass factory. In the middle of July 1908, a public meeting was called and he was asked to outline his plans. Several committees were formed by those present, plans were studied, and the Fenton plant at Williamstown was visited. Eleven days later a second meeting was held to finalize plans for the glass plant. Options on land were quickly okayed, methods of lot selling were discussed and finalized. (The actual selling of lots began in mid-August on a 54.7 acre parcel of land on the north edge of Millersburg.)

There has always been speculation that some sort of connection between the Williamstown plant and the Millersburg plant existed, but from all we can learn, this was just not the case. We believe some members of the Fenton family personally put funds behind brother John but nothing else.

On September 14, 1908, ground was broken for the glass factory and John Fenton's hopes were about to be realized. Like his dreams, it was to be the grandest glass plant ever, with a main building that was 300 feet by 100 feet, spanned by steel framework with no center supports, and featuring a well-planned work area. An adjoining building, 50 by 300 feet, was used for a packing and storage area, a cooper shop (to produce packaging and barrels), and a tool shop. The main building also

John W. Fenton and H.F. Weber in the office of the Millersburg Glass Company. The calender on the wall behind them is dated April 1909.

housed the work area, a mixing room, a lehr area, office space, and a display area for samples of the glass. While construction progressed, John Fenton canvassed the area, selling stock, acting as a promotions man, and overlooking the drilling of gas wells to deliver a source of fuel to the plant. (Eighteen wells are said to have been drilled, with John Fenton eyeballing most of them.) At the same time, stocks of $100.00 shares, totalling $125,000.00 were issued. Upon incorporation, John Fenton became company president, H.W. Stanley vice-president and treasurer, Robert Fenton (John and Frank L.'s brother) secretary, and H.F. Weber general sales manager.

Finally, on May 20, 1909, the first glass was poured and the next weekend visitors were welcomed to the plant where glass samples were handed to everyone. (Lucille Lowe once wrote these gifts were Ohio Star toothpick holders in crystal.) Initial pourings were of two well-known patterns, accord-

Millersburg postcard showing the factory in progress and John Fenton's message and signature on the reverse side.
Courtesy of Steve Maag.

8

MASSIVE "SUNFLOWER AND LEAF" DESIGN PUNCH SET.

It's equal in quality and design never priced as low.

1C1983—Diam. deep bowl 15½ ht. with separate stand 13, brilliant extra heavy pressed crystal, finest fire polish, twin sunflower panels with prominent leaves, deep notched scallop edge; 12 full size handled cups. 1 set in pkg. Per set, **$2.35**

1C1984—Allover fired golden iridescent finish, otherwise as 1C1983. 1 set in pkg. Per set, **$2.95**

Millersburg ad for the Hobstar and Feather punch set in the October 1909 Butler Brothers catalog.

ing to most sources; these were Hobstar and Feather pieces and Ohio Star items. (The very first ad in the Butler Brothers catalog is a Hobstar and Feather cracker jar with cover in crystal at 32 cents each and described as a "Massive Covered Cracker Jar with deep cut sunburst and encircling leaf design.")

John Fenton, in his usual promotional way promised the visitors that many other wares were on the horizon, including opal glass and novelty items. John's daughter, Nellie Fenton Glasgo, recalled in 1981 that her father had designed both of these patterns, just as he had designed others at the Williamstown firm, including one bowl pattern that bore the profile of her mother (obviously the Goddess of Harvest bowl). The glass was top quality crystal and was the mainstay at Millersburg for about two months, but soon iridized items emerged using the original Fenton process. The first colors were green and amethyst, with a mellow marigold following a few weeks later.

The first ad in Butler Brothers that showed iridized Millersburg glass was in October 1909. It was the Hobstar and Feather punch set, offered in crystal or "all over fired golden iridescent finish." Other Millersburg ads in the same issue offered a three-piece (assorted shapes) grouping of Potpourri compotes in crystal at 89 cents per dozen. Surprisingly there was a separate ad for the Venetian punch set in crystal! This ad appeared long after the Ohio Flint Glass Company had ended so we may well speculate just who was advertising this set. It had to be either Jefferson Glass who had bought the moulds from the Ohio Flint or Millersburg who had bought the moulds from Jefferson earlier that year. There is no evidence to support Jefferson ever having made either Venetian or Honeycomb and Hobstar and we know by this time Millersburg already owned the Colonial or Flute moulds with the clover-leaf base. John Fenton had struck a deal with Jefferson for these moulds after Jefferson bought all the "Krys-tol" trademark moulds at Ohio Flint's demise. These moulds included the Chippendale line which Jefferson very much wanted to own, the Gloria moulds which are called Honeycomb and Hobstar by carnival collectors, and the Kenneth moulds which are now Venetian (as well as the Colonial or Flute moulds). John Fenton needed moulds and the deal was consummated. In addition, he purchased several new moulds from the Hipkins Novelty Mould Company that included the Cherry design (it soon became a leader in sales), and other moulds that included Country Kitchen, its variant Potpourri, and the "wreath" patterns, Blackberry, Grape, and Strawberry. At about the same time we surmise he also purchased the Riverside lamp moulds that included Wild Rose, Ladies' Medal-

"MAMMOTH" GLASS PITCHER.
Extra size—striking design—low priced.

C586—Mammoth low shape, ht. 8, girth 22½, capacity 3½ qts., extra heavy sparkling crystal, massive sunburst and leaf panel base, plain top. 1 in pkg.
Each. **37c**

"Variety Design" Bonbon Dishes.

1C460—4 shapes—diamond, club, heart, spade, about 5 in. diam., crystal, sunburst medallions within leaf wreaths. 1 doz. in box, asstd.................................Doz. **39c**

"EXTRA LARGE" NEW DESIGN CRYSTAL VASES.
Rich attractive mold, distinct new design. Ornament on any table and placed within reach of all.

1C587—Ht. 9 in., diam. 7 in. cupped mammoth flower mold, scallop top, extra heavy fine crystal, prominent deep cut sunflower and serpentine leaf design, flaring sunflower cut base. 1 in pkg.
Each, **34c**
1C600—As 1C587, green, iridescent. 1 in pkg.
Each, **36c**

"MASSIVE" COVERED CRACKER JAR.
A genuine cut facsimile at a "never equalled" price. Just glance at it.

1C585: Mammoth covered shapes, 6¾ x6¾, extra heavy brilliant finish crystal, deep cut sunburst and encircling leaf design. 1 in pkg.
Each. **32c**

"VARIETY DESIGN" OLIVE OR BONBON DISHES.
A collection of sellers—the special price allows an extra profit.

1C461—4 shapes—diamond, club, heart, spade, diam. about 5 in., practical sizes, extra brilliant crystal, large sunburst medallions within leaf wreaths, distinct notched edges. 1 doz. in box, asstd.
Per dozen, **36c**

Various Hobstar and Feather ads in Butler Brothers catalogs, beginning in October 1909, and continuing through 1912. Note: The Hobstar and Feather bridge set pieces (olive or bonbon dishes) changed price from 36¢ in the first ad to 39¢ in the next.

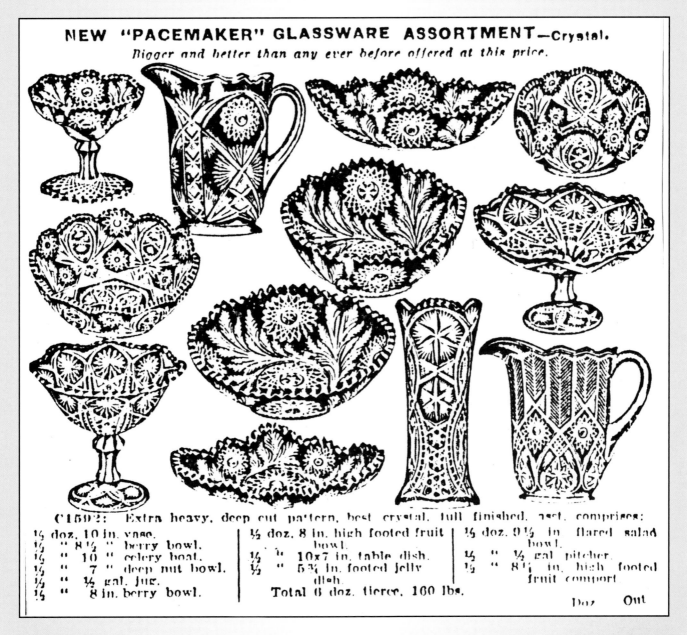

Butler Brothers catalog ad in 1911, featuring an assortment of Millersburg crystal pieces. These include Marilyn pitchers, Feather and Heart pitchers, Ohio Star vase, Potpourri compote and salver, Hobstar and Feather compote, bowls, pickle dish, and banana boat, and Near-Cut Wreath bowl and rose bowl (strangely, none of these bowls or rose bowls in this pattern have been reported today).

A February 1911, Butler Brothers catalog ad showing an assortment of Millersburg table sets in crystal, in Flute, Ohio Star, Hobstar and Feather, and Country Kitchen.

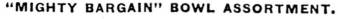

"MIGHTY BARGAIN" BOWL ASSORTMENT.
Extraordinary value. Regular jobbing price 89c.

C2151: Full finished crystal, aver. diam. 8¾ in., 3 brilliant patterns—star and leaf, fan and diamond, and star and diamond cuttings. 2 doz. each, 6 doz. bbl. ——— lbs.   Doz. **72c**

An April 1911, Butler Brothers Millersburg ad showing an assortment of Millersburg crystal bowls in Fine-cut Hearts, Cactus, and Mayflower, all exterior patterns.

Butler Brothers catalog ad, 1909 – 1912, showing the Potpourri compotes and salver in crystal.

HIGH FOOTED SALVER AND FRUIT BOWL ASST.—(Crystal)

Excellent patterns — items that sell every day in the year. Unmatchable at this price.

C1567—Good crystal, brilliant star and jeweled panel design, fire polish. Comprises: 2 doz. footed bowls, diam. 7½, round and crimped shapes. 1 doz. 9 in. cake salvers. Total 3 doz. bbl. 112 lbs.   Doz. **92c**

"MARATHON" JUG ASST.
The kind that has always jobbed at $2.00 dozen.

C2121: 2 styles, full finished crystal, so called ½ gal., 8¼ in. tall, 1½ doz. each deep daisy and fan, and feather and star cutting. 3 doz. tierce.   Doz. **$1.10**

A Butler Brothers ad that has caused some confusion with glass collectors who have sometimes believed the compote on the left was the Ohio Star tall jelly compote. It isn't. This is a McKee "Prescut" ad that shows a Sextec compote on the right and the disputed Yutec compote on the left. This compote is probably the one advertised before John Fenton designed Ohio Star that has contributed to some collectors saying the Ohio Star pattern predates the Millersburg Company.

Butler Brothers ad, April 1912, showing both the Marilyn and Feather and Heart water pitchers in crystal.

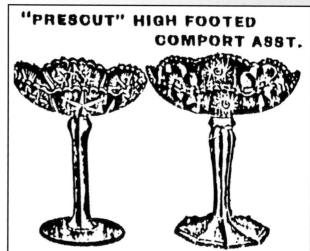

"PRESCUT" HIGH FOOTED COMPORT ASST.

1C1760—Diam. 6¼ in., ht. 7½ in., colonial stem foot, 1½ doz. each 2 cut designs, brilliant finish, fire polish. 3 doz. in bbl., 81 lbs.   Doz. **95c**

lion, and Colonial patterns.

Early shapes produced at Millersburg were primarily useful ones such as water sets, table sets (butter dish with cover, sugar bowl with cover, cream jug, and spooner or spoonholder), cracker jars, toothpick holders, cruets, syrup jugs, bowls, and salt and pepper shakers. Also listed on early inventory records is an ale glass (where is one?). In addition, two large punch bowls, stands, and matching cups were made in the Hobstar and Feather and the Ohio Star patterns (these were numbered Millersburg's 358 and 353 respectively). But in early ads the Hobstar and Feather pattern was called "sunflower and leaf" or "sunflower and serpentine," while the company name for the 353 patterns was actually Ohio Star.

January of 1910 gave birth to the celebrated line of iridized glass known as Radium and marked the high point of the Millersburg plant. Radium was a softer shade of base color with a watery, mirror-like iridescence that was said to glow and sparkle with a life of its own. Oliver Phillips is credited with the radium process and when the new finish was unveiled at a Pittsburgh Glass Show

China, Glass and Lamps Catalog cover.

on January 15, 1910, it drew instant attention. A *China, Glass and Lamps* publication ad of that time describes Radium as "the latest Triumph in the Glass Industry," and continues: "Radium sends out all the sparkling effects of that wonderful mineral." It continues, "The glass is Chameleon" and the "premier of Iridescent Ware." The ad lists H.F. Weber and J.W. Fenton as company representatives at the Fort Pitt Hotel, Rooms 543 and 544. The pieces that drew the attention of the crowds seem to have been either the Big Fish or Trout and Fly patterns, as well as the Nesting Swan design. Another ad from two weeks later lists the same two representatives at the same hotel in rooms 688, 543 – 544, so more space must have been needed. The fish pattern displayed was said to "glow" and look as if it were about to "leap" from the bowl. Following the success of the Pittsburgh show, it was decided that the glass line needed to be expanded. Business was good, large orders were coming in, and glass journals were excited about Radium. More ad space was purchased. In the February 19, 1910, *Pottery, Glass, and Brass Salesman* an ad appeared that showed the sun rising over water with the narrative that read: "As an exhibition of alternating and intermingling colors, the grandest rainbow ever seen in eastern sky has nothing on Radium Glass — A different iridescent effect is produced on every individual piece. Radium is an art glass for the masses

— if you cater to them get in touch with us. Radium will double your sales. Hundreds of articles for every practical purpose you expect to find in glass...." It was signed Millersburg Glass Company, Millersburg, Ohio.

Additional moulds were ordered from Hipkins, and in June, the famous Courthouse bowl was produced, reputedly as a gesture of appreciation for those who had laid the gas lines from the wells to the factory. After some pouring of glass on this piece, it was decided to add "Millersburg, Ohio" below the courthouse scene and the mould was retooled. The so-called unlettered examples are much rarer today and bring considerably higher prices. The Courthouse bowls are all in amethyst Radium but a few have a softer mauve coloring. Shapes known are an ice cream shaped bowl, a six-ruffle bowl, or a three-in-one edged bowl. Other examples of John Fenton's generosity are the crystal Ohio Star punch sets he furnished each of the churches in Millersburg, and of course, the famous People's Vase (listed on the inventory sheets as "Holland vase #70") which we are told was designed to honor the Amish of the area. In fact, hardly any visitor to the Millersburg factory during this time came away without a souvenir piece of glass of one kind or another.

Once the additional labor forces were hired. John Fenton proceeded to buy new moulds. Peacocks were in vogue as a design element and not to be outdone by his competitors, it is said he purchased several live peacocks and hens, turning them loose on the factory grounds for the mould designers to study. It must have worked for the numerous peacock designs from Millersburg are among the best around. (Area residents were not so happy about the whole affair, however, and often complained about the noise the birds caused, especially during the evening and night hours.)

John Fenton and the rest of his family were often involved in community endeavors and one is remembered more than any other. During an annual festival, the Fentons provided an elaborate float wagon, heavily decorated with bunting, and complete with crystal Ohio Star punch bowls from which young ladies in costume passed out samples to the crowds. The wagon was pulled by a company vehicle, also decked out with American flags. Behind them marched a gayly bedecked band. All went well until some of the townspeople learned John Fenton had spiked the punch! The town's leaders were incensed and told Mr. Fenton so, and while he gave them his apologies, it was some time

Photo of the infamous punch wagon John Fenton provided for the July 4, 1909, Millersburg parade. Punch was served from Ohio Star punch bowls (three on each side of the wagon). Photo courtesy of Don Doyle, Rockford, Illinois.

before the incident was either forgiven or forgotten. It was about this time, Robert Fenton, secretary of the corporation, left Millersburg to return to his old job with the railroad at Marion, Ohio. This was not a permanent move and within a short time Frank L. had lured him to Williamstown where he began a career with the Fenton Art Glass Company.

Postcard of the mixing room at Millersburg Glass Company. From author's collection.

In December of 1910, the *Pottery, Glass, and Brass Salesman* journal reported John Fenton was introducing extensive improvements at the factory and a sizable expansion plan was in progress. At the same time, additional pattern moulds were ordered from Hipkins which included Peacock Tail Variant, Multi-Fruits and Flowers moulds, Rosalind, Whirling Leaves, and Primrose moulds. Factory hours were extended and a contract was awarded to a Pittsburgh firm to install a new wind system that would clean the air. Some of the interior photos of the factory show the elaborate ductwork that spans the building's ceilings. At the same time, skilled workers were sought and the manpower of the plant nearly doubled. It was as if John Fenton knew he had problems but believed he could spend them away. In only a few weeks, the factory was closed because of a lawsuit by Hipkins in January 1911. It was temporary and the factory reopened in late February with (according to John Fenton) enough orders and re-orders to keep everyone busy for months. Every effort was made to assure the townspeople that all was clear sailing. But Hipkins had been trying to collect mould bills for nearly two years. A judgment was reached in March (in Hipkins' favor) and by this time

Millersburg Glass Company stock certificate dated 1910.

other creditors came forward and the floodgates opened. Petitioners included the American Iron and Supply Company, Fairbanks Morse and Company, and even the People's National Bank of Millersburg. In addition stockholders and lot buyers were heard about their complaints and in all, about 20 suits were filed. The Millersburg Glass Company had no choice but to face receivership with bankruptcy only a few days away.

Despite the many problems, John Fenton never stopped assuring the townspeople the plant would soon be re-opening, but a court-ordered inventory and several attempts to sell the facility brought no relief until Samuel B. Fair stepped forward and bought the factory and all assets in late September or early October for slightly more than $14,000.00 (less than half of the appraised value of $32,500.00). Mr. Fair was the Holmes County treasurer and a novice in the glass business. He had been one of the original owners of the land that had been purchased for the factory site, and now he felt the factory needed to be saved because of its importance to the economy of Millersburg. Fair quickly formed the Radium Glass Company, and informed everyone he would be using Millersburg moulds and Millersburg employees to make Radium glass once again. With a new crew of John Moritz as shop manager, C.J. Fisher as secretary, M.V. Legillon as treasurer, John Fenton as vice-president (this is a move we still question today and no real reason has ever come to light), and himself as president.

The Radium Glass Company began production in mid-November, using Millersburg moulds and even adding a few of their own, notably the Boutonniere and Rosalind compotes. The factory operated until June of 1912 when it closed for a second time. John Fenton had departed under a shadow earlier in the year but continued to be a resident of Millersburg, along with his family. In late May, the final shipment of glass left the factory, bound for the Woolworth Company. Workers were instructed to fill no more orders although large amounts of finished glass remained on hand. Samuel Fair, like many investors, lost most of his worldly assets in the closing. His daughter, Mary Fair Hoffman, vividly recalled the long lean years when this author spoke with her in 1981 shortly before her death, and the same tale of hardship was told by John Fenton's daughter, Nellie Fenton Glasco. Both credited faith and closeness of family in their recovery.)

As for John Fenton, it must have been equally as painful. His personality was simply not geared for failure. He is known to have been involved in a variety of sales jobs, traveling at one time or another as a jobber, selling advertising, but always trying to get his name back before the glassmakers and buyers. (From time to time brief narratives would appear in glass journals telling of a new venture in the glass world but we suspect these were mostly planted by him to keep his name in the wind.) His eldest daughter died of influenza in 1918, his wife was killed in an auto accident in 1921 when she was swept from an open touring car onto a road as the vehicle swerved to avoid an oncoming truck driven, ironically, by Samuel Fair's son. Two of John's children had passed on in infancy and only two daughters, Helen Fenton Elliot and Nellie Fenton Glasco remained. At one point in time, John Fenton was living over a drugstore and needed medicine. He carried a carnival vase to the druggist and requested a trade, the druggist obliged, then set the vase on a shelf in the back. This vase was later purchased from the store just where it had been sitting all those years by the late Evelyn Guest of Canton, Ohio. It turned out to be one of the rare Honeycomb and Hobstar carnival glass vases. At one time John Fenton was reported to have been peddling his ideas for a new type of flying machine. It had a large rotating propeller on the top, just like present-day helicopters! So the dreams went on until John passed away in January 1934. He is buried in Oak Hill Cemetery in Millersburg.

After more than a year in idleness, the factory was sold to Jefferson Glass and Frank Sinclair in October 1913. Sinclair was an organizer and now a mover with Jefferson of Stuebenville, Ohio (founded in 1901, the company moved to Follansbee, West Virginia, in 1907, and remained active until 1933). In 1908 Jefferson bought the "Krys-tol" line from closing Ohio Flint Glass. Once again glass was to be poured at Millersburg, but only for lighting glass ware, consisting of lantern, reflector, auto lights, and railroad lighting items. The moulds still remained at Millersburg and many were scrapped or sold. The large compote/vase shape for the Venetian pattern was sold to Cambridge and it became a crystal lamp base as their #2340 lamp.) Several moulds were retained and shipped to the Jefferson Glass Company, Limited, plant at Toronto, Canada, and are shown in company glass cata-

Entrance sign to Oak Hill Cemetery of Millersburg, Ohio, where John Fenton and his family are buried. The sign says "Village of Millersburg." Courtesy of John Calai.

Fenton gravesite in Millersburg at the Oak Hill Cemetery. John's daughter, Grace, is on the left, his wife Quindiara is in the middle, and John is on the right. Courtesy of John Calai.

logs from there. These are Hobstar and Feather moulds (Jefferson's #358) in berry sets, table sets, a stemmed dessert, and the punch set; as well as Ohio Star (Jefferson's #353) in the punch set, and the Flute moulds (originally Ohio Flint's) in the two sizes of clover-based compotes, and the blank for the Big Thistle punch set with no interior pattern. These, along with a round-based open or covered compote are all listed as Jefferson's #1600 pattern(s). All were listed only in crystal.

Production at Millersburg was brief for Jefferson's lighting division and in the fall of 1916 the operation was moved back to Follansbee, West Virginia. The fixtures and furnishings were removed from the plant, the great stack was dismantled, and in 1919 the building was sold to the Forrester Tire and Rubber Company. Since that time various owners have come and gone and for a while, the plant served in the making of school bus units. A parking lot has been added in front of the factory and when we saw it in 1999, the building looked in good repair and well kept.

We haven't been able to learn just how much crystal was produced in Canada using the Millersburg moulds. Jefferson operated the plant in Toronto until 1925, primarily as a producer of electric bulbs, lamps, globes, and other lighting wares. Their operation was large, with a 16-pot furnace (gas), operating night and day. On occasion, one sees a piece of Ohio Star or Hobstar and Feather in crystal that looks different (not as clear or brilliant) and we have to wonder if it is Canadian. The Canadian line of #1600 Flute or Colonial from Jefferson is huge and looks as if it may be a composite line from all their Flute patterns. Still the two known Millersburg clover-base compotes can't be ignored as part of it. Perhaps we'll never know the full story. One has to wonder whatever happened to the Hobstar and Feather and Ohio Star moulds, the two patterns that started our remarkable story.

In recent years, many shards have been recovered by area Millersburg collectors, and while we realize these do not tell a complete story, some very interesting surprises have surfaced. In 1999, at the Millersburg Festival, we were privileged to examine some of these shards and saw first-hand some previously unreported patterns and glass treatments. These include parts of a Cherry powder jar in milk glass that looked iridized; blue opaque shards from a Potpourri compote (we were told an intact example of this piece exists); one handled shard that was emerald green and had a casing of milk glass; also, there were soft yellow shards, purple slag pieces of glass, green slag items, and even a couple of shards of milk glass with a heavy marigold iridescence. We have known for some time that John Fenton was experimenting with new glass treatments all the time; Frank M. Fenton confirmed this in a conversation we had some years ago. He had produced the Country Kitchen variant with flint opalescent treatment and examples of these are well known. In addition, Hobstar and Feather pieces, while very rare, can be found in a ruby stain treatment (examples include a 5½" square mint dish, a covered sugar, a spooner, and a bridge set club piece that is in the Fenton Museum). In addition, examples of a cranberry staining commonly called "Maiden Blush" are known. I own one and it also has gilding on the edges. In addition, several uniridized pieces in color are in collections. These include a Swirl Hobnail spittoon and a Diamonds tumbler in amethyst; an Ohio Star compote, Potpourri compote, and a Hobstar and Feather pickle dish, all in sapphire blue glass. Some of the shards reveal patterns here-to-fore not suspected to be from Millersburg. These include the

Woodpecker and Ivy vase and the Butterfly and Corn vase. Both of these patterns are very rare with only two or three examples of each known.

In another area, we now know that when the Riverside Glass Company of Wellsburg, West Virginia, closed John Fenton purchased their lamp series called the "Lucille line," consisting of the Ladies' Medallion lamp, the Wild Rose lamp, and a paneled version without the foliage called the Colonial Variant. John Fenton had these retooled, removing the "Riverside Clinch-on Collar" lettering (on most) and made these lamps in iridized glass. Some pieces were produced in crystal and in this book we are pleased to show both the handled Wild Rose lamp and the handled Colonial lamp, neither shown in any of the Millersburg books before. We strongly suspect both the Ladies' Medallion (Riverside called this the Riverside Ladies lamp) and the regular Wild Rose lamp may have been made in crystal without removing the lettering from Riverside since a marigold carnival lamp is known with the lettering still on it. In addition, we strongly suspect that both the Honeycomb and Hobstar (Gloria) and the Venetian (Kenneth) patterns were made in crystal at the Millersburg plant. Most of these pieces are found marked (Krys-tol or Crys-tal) but the clover-based 6" compote in carnival glass also bears the latter mark so we know it was put into production in iridized glass without removing the marking. We may never know how many of these pieces were made at Ohio Flint or even at Millersburg but I do know there is certainly room for speculation about some production at the latter plant. Finally, some of these moulds from the Kenneth and Gloria patterns were purchased by the Central Glass Company, once the Millersburg plant closed and were used in their production of crystal items.

In 1981, when I was writing the first Millersburg crystal book, I interviewed both Mary Fair Hoffman, Samuel Fair's daughter, and Nellie Fenton Glasgo, John Fenton's daughter. Both were very helpful and were very keen mentally, considering they were well along in life. I remember asking Nellie Glasgo why her father made so many variations of a pattern, specifically the Peacock, and Peacock and Urn patterns, and she smiled and told me what she called the "family secret." She said her father was a good mould designer but couldn't really imagine what the piece was going to look like until he held the finished product in his hand. So it appears he made an example, decided it needed small changes, made another and instituted even more changes. Today, all these variations are what intrigue us most about Millersburg glass, and as every year passes, we learn a little more about these variations, about John Fenton and how he made glass his way. The remarkable results and the wonderful glass his peculiarities produced are feats that all of us have come to respect over the years. If only the company could have stayed in business. If only more records had been preserved. If only even more patterns had been born. . . life is filled with "if onlys." But rather than thinking about those, we must be thankful for John Fenton, for his glass, and for the citizens of Millersburg who have preserved his contributions, so that all of us can see and hold these remarkable feats that a man and his vision produced.

Present day views of the Millersburg factory showing the original building remains as well as additions, presently used by IPS.

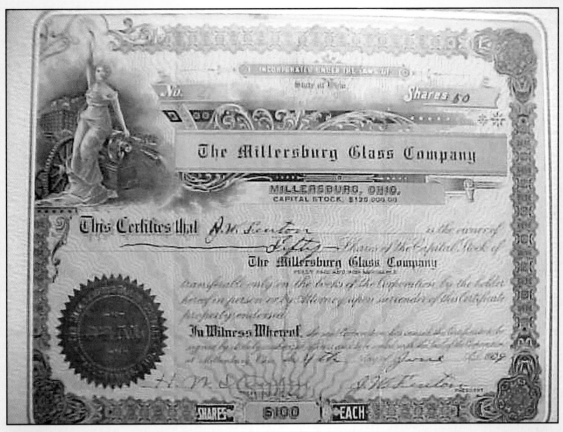

Stock certificates that were signed by John W. Fenton and purchased by him. The other signature is that of H.W. Stanley, prominent Marietta, Ohio, businessman who was in the furniture business with his partner, Charles Grass.

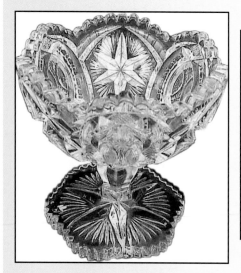

Ohio Star compote.

Hobstar and Feather cracker jar with lid.

Hobstar and Feather
rose bowl whimsey
(from jelly compote),
frosted feathers.

Ohio Star 5¼" square
dish with gold.

Hobstar and Feather 6" x 5" mint dish
with ruby stain.

Diamond Amethyst tumbler.

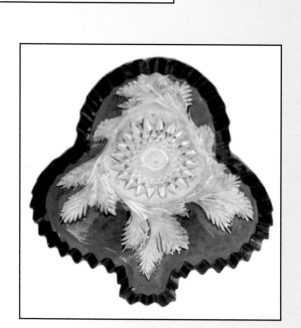

Hobstar and Feather club piece
in ruby stain. Courtesy of Fenton Museum.

Millersburg Glass Shards

In recent years, several Millersburg-area collectors have spent many hours digging at the Millersburg factory site and have uncovered some interesting items. The following photos are a few samples of these remarkable finds that include a milk glass Cherry powder jar lid, bits of opaque blue glass, chunks of green slag, uniridized hunks of purple glass in the Flute pattern, pieces of iridized milk glass, parts of sapphire blue Ohio Star and Potpourri items, a chunk of purple slag, and of course, many bits of carnival glass in recognizable patterns in marigold, green, amethyst, white, and even peach opalescent carnival glass.

We express our thanks to John Calai, Sonny Hall, Larry Cullen, and all the others who have spent long hours in liberating these shards. We have to go back in history to Lucille Lowe who pioneered this search and who showed me the first pieces of the People's Vase in amethyst she had dug three decades ago.

Shards do not give all the answers but they go a long way toward dispelling the myths that have grown over the years. In some instances, like the finding of the Woodpecker and Ivy, as well as the Butterfly and Corn shards, they open new vistas for the researcher as well as the collector.

We are happy to show a few of these finds here and express our thanks to those who labored to recover them.

A broken Millersburg Cherry lid from the powder jar in milk glass that was dug from the factory site by a local collector.

Millersburg Glass Shards

Millersburg Cherry shards in green slag with an opaque lining. This treatment hasn't been found on a complete item so we can surmise these pieces were experimental.

A large chunk of a green shard that shows some iridization. The pattern is Hobstar and Feather.

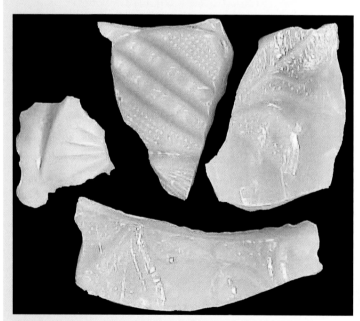

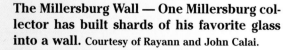

Shards of an opaque blue glass that were unearthed at the Millersburg plant site. Note that the color is almost like Fenton's Persian Blue opaque glass.

The Millersburg Wall — One Millersburg collector has built shards of his favorite glass into a wall. Courtesy of Rayann and John Calai.

Jefferson Glass Company Limited

of Toronto, Canada

The following pages show Millersburg Glass Company patterns that were produced at the Jefferson Glass Company factory in Toronto, Canada, in 1915 – 1916. We have always been grateful to our dear friends, Syd and Ola Shoom for providing these pages of the catalog to us and they were also published in a fine book by Gerald Stevens called *Canadian Glass, 1825 – 1925* (published 1979, Cole Publishing Company, Toronto, Canada).

MADE IN CANADA

CATALOGUE No. 21.

Illustrating

TABLEWARE & TUMBLERS
LAMPS *and* FOUNTS & SODA
FOUNTAIN SUPPLIES *and*
SUNDRY PRESSED WARE.

JEFFERSON GLASS COMPANY, LIMITED
Head Office *and* Factory - 388 Carlaw Ave.
TORONTO

Catalog cover showing Millersburg Glass Company patterns.

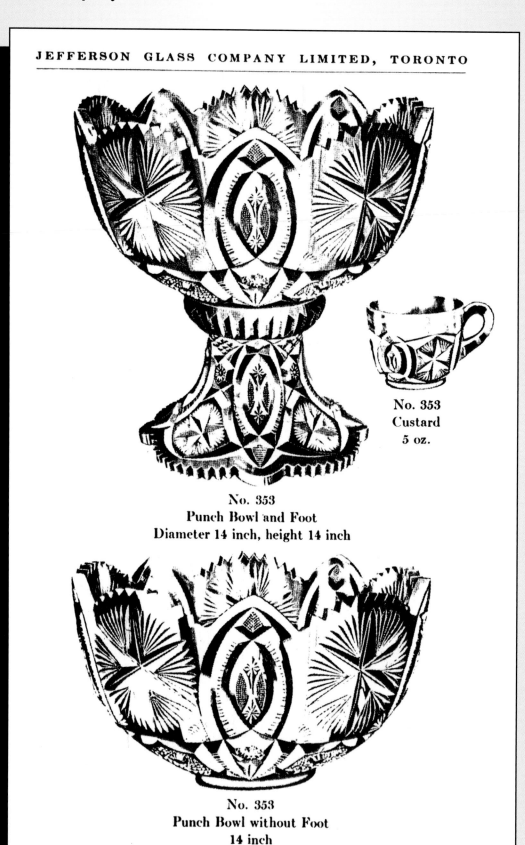

JEFFERSON GLASS COMPANY LIMITED, TORONTO

No. 353
Custard
5 oz.

No. 353
Punch Bowl and Foot
Diameter 14 inch, height 14 inch

No. 353
Punch Bowl without Foot
14 inch

Ohio Star punch bowl, base, cup.

JEFFERSON GLASS COMPANY LIMITED, TORONTO

No. 358
Punch Bowl and Foot
Diameter 15 inch, height 13 inch

No. 358
Punch Bowl without Foot
15 inch

Hobstar and Feather punch bowl, base.

JEFFERSON GLASS COMPANY LIMITED, TORONTO

No. 358
Butter and Cover

No. 358—FOUR-PIECE TEA SET

No. 358
Cream
11 oz.

No. 358
Spoon

No. 358
Sugar and Cover

HOBSTAR & FEATHER table set pieces

Hobstar and Feather table set pieces.

JEFFERSON GLASS COMPANY LIMITED, TORONTO

No. 358
Custard
6 oz.

No. 358
Sundae
5 oz.

No. 358
Nappy
4½ inch

No. 358
Orange Dish
11 inch

No. 358
Nappy
8½ inch

Hobstar and Feather assorted items.

JEFFERSON GLASS COMPANY LIMITED, TORONTO

No. 1600
Punch Bowl and Foot
12 inch

No. 1600
Punch Bowl without Foot
12 inch

Millersburg Flute (Colonial) punch bowl and base.

JEFFERSON GLASS COMPANY LIMITED, TORONTO

No. 1600—INDIVIDUAL CREAM AND SUGAR SET

No. 1600
Individual Sugar

No. 1600
Individual Cream

No. 1600—HOTEL CREAM AND SUGAR SET

No. 1600
Hotel Sugar

No. 1600
Hotel Cream

No. 1600—5 oz.
Mustard and Cover

No. 1600—16 oz.
Syrup

JEFFERSON GLASS COMPANY LIMITED, TORONTO

No. 1600
High-Footed Bowl, Scalloped
7 and 8 inch
No. 2 Finish

No. 1600
High-Footed Bowl, Scalloped
5 inch
No. 1 Finish

No. 1600
High-Footed Bowl, Plain
7 and 8 inch
No. 2 Finish

No. 1600
High-Footed Bowl
With Cover
7 and 8 inch

Millersburg Flute (Colonial) compotes.

Millersburg Exterior Bowl Patterns

Nearly every one of the fine exterior patterns found on Millersburg carnival bowls are also found on crystal bowls as the primary pattern. The exception to this is the Finecut Ovals pattern and we suspect it was made and will someday show up. The rest: Cactus, Diamond and Fan, Fine Cut Heart, Mayflower, Trefoil Finecut, and Near Cut Wreath are all known or shown in old Millersburg ads in Butler Brothers catalogs. Add to these the Country Kitchen, and the two Flute or Wide Panel designs and you have every Millersburg exterior pattern on bowls.

All of these patterns are rare in crystal and many collectors haven't seen more than one or two. Trefoil Finecut, Cactus, and Fine Cut Heart are the most often found with only about 6 – 12 of each reported. And while it was well advertised, we know of only 2 – 3 Mayflower bowls; and despite being shown in ads in a bowl and a rose bowl shape, we know of no collectors who report owning an example of Near Cut Wreath, so where are they? The Diamond and Fan bowl shown here is the first reported example so these must be very rare too.

Each of these exterior designs is a very distinctive pattern and are some of the best patterns ever devised for bowls. All are unique in one way or another and all show interesting base or marie designs, making them stand-outs when displayed. The glass is generally of fine fire-polished quality, especially on the Mayflower and Fine Cut Heart bowls; the Cactus has been reported with a dull glass look but the ones we've seen (only two) have been top quality. And while Trefoil Finecut is probably the most sought, the Mayflower has to be the stand-out as far as beauty and rarity.

We'd certainly like to hear from anyone who has an example of either Near Cut Wreath or Finecut Ovals. We've searched long and hard for a piece of the former to show in this book but haven't had any luck.

Cactus

Shown is the rare 9" bowl in crystal, the only shape reported in this pattern. The pattern is all exterior and in carnival glass it is the secondary pattern for Rays and Ribbons. We don't have a count on this pattern but believe there are no more than a dozen crystal examples known. Cactus is shown as late as April 1912, in the Butler Brothers catalog in a Millersburg crystal ad that features three bowls: Cactus, Mayflower, and Finecut Hearts. It is listed as "full finished crystal" (the ad terms for the patterns are "star and leaf," "star and diamond," and "fan and diamond" patterns). Some of the known examples of Cactus seem to be found on a duller glass than one would expect from Millersburg but there is no evidence anyone else ever made this pattern. The Cactus design is a series of fan-shaped leaves with needles on the edges, with a hobstar centered above and between each leaf-fan. The base (marie) is a section of cactus or leaves that fan in a circle from the center and completely fill the circle. $400.00.

Diamond and Fan

Normally found as the exterior secondary pattern on Nesting Swan bowls in carnival glass, this very rare bowl is shown for the first time in crystal. The design is a series of diamonds, fans, and reverse fans, arranged in rows that seem to grow outward from the marie, which has a prismed diamond star that is edged with fans. The bowl shown is a deep round shape that is 8" across, but since Nesting Swan bowls are known in several shapes that include six-ruffled, square and tri-cornered with candy-ribbon edging, and even a spittoon whimsey, anything is possible with crystal items. $500.00, rare.

Fine Cut Heart

Normally found in iridized glass as the exterior pattern on Primrose bowls, Fine Cut Heart is found rarely in crystal on 9½" – 10" bowls. The crystal pieces were first advertised in a Butler Brothers catalog in 1910 and were still being shown in the April 1912 edition of the same catalog. All examples seem to be full finished crystal that was polished indicating it was for a better trade. The design is a good one, covering a lot of space without being overpowering, and the collectibility is near the top with only a handful of these known. $400.00.

Mayflower

Here is a bowl that has to be at the top of Millersburg patterns for exterior bowl pieces. In carnival glass it is found as the secondary or exterior pattern for the rare Grape Leaves bowls, and in crystal it is just as rare. To date the example shown is the only one we've heard about. Mayflower is a series of flower-like designs separated by eight diamond and near-cut sections. The effect between the flowers looks like feathers of herringbone, and on the marie, the same herringbone sections fan out from the center dividing fanned sections of diamond filing. The crystal is sparkling and clear and this bowl should be rated as the top in its class. $500.00, rare.

Trefoil Finecut

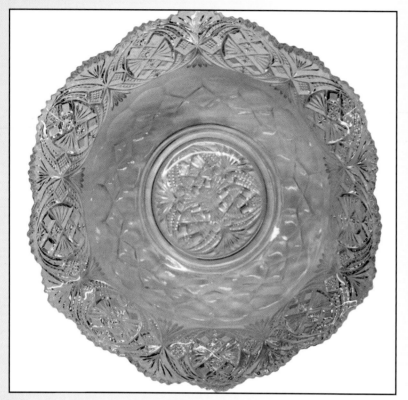

Found on all carnival glass Many Stars bowls as the secondary (exterior) pattern, Trefoil Finecut is also found on a very, very rare marigold chop plate as the *only* pattern. On the few existing crystal bowls, the shape is usually six-ruffled and about 9" – 9½" in diameter with a depth of 2½" to 3". The design is an interesting one with two rings of unrelated design. The outer ring is a series of ovals that are filled with diamonds, diamond starbursts, and fans while separating each of the ovals is a sunburst of fans and file-filled diamonds. The second row of design is a honeycombing that is typical of Millersburg patterns. The marie or base has a triangle of the same ovals, separated by three sections of fans. Bowl, $475.00. Plate, $800.00, rare.

Photo of the bowl from the side.

Gallery of Glass

Country Kitchen

Just why John Fenton decided to produce two variations of a pattern is unclear but surely he must have had a practical reason. First advertised as a "star and jewel panel" pattern, it is obvious the Country Kitchen, County Kitchen Variant (Milky Way), and the Potpourri patterns were virtually interchangeable in the same ads. We now know the Country Kitchen Variant is found mostly in opalescent treatment but is known in crystal as well. In addition, in this book we show a bowl in the regular Country Kitchen with an opalescent edge, so there doesn't seem to be much of a separation between these variants.

Ads call these pieces "fire polished heavy crystal" and most pieces are just that with a sparkling clarity that is as good as the Ohio Star pieces. The Potpourri differs from the other designs in that it features a pinwheel of daisies around a hobstar.

Country Kitchen Covered Butter Dish

Here is the very scarce butter dish, found more often in carnival glass than crystal. It has a prism-type lid knob and the well-known design over most of the rest of the space. The glass is very clear and polished. $200.00

Country Kitchen Creamer

Fire polished and sparkling, this creamer is rare in crystal but, shows the design to its very best advantage. Few of these are reported despite being advertised in Butler Brothers catalog in 1911. $75.00.

Country Kitchen Covered Sugar

One of Millersburg's prettiest table sets, this piece is just plain attractive from all angles. The glass is polished to a high glow and the design seems just right for the shapes. All pieces in the table set are quite hard to find in crystal, especially the butter dish. $150.00.

Country Kitchen Plate

Apparently this was a favored pattern at the Millersburg plant and only the Hobstar and Feather and Ohio Star patterns are known in more shapes in crystal. Here we show a 12" plate but plates in Country Kitchen are also found in 5", 7", and 9½" sizes. An early Butler Brothers ad showing this pattern says it was a "full finished crystal pattern," indicating it had been polished piece by piece and by hand. This was an extra step to indicate the pattern was top of the line. 5", $65.00; 7", $75.00; 10", $85.00; 12", $100.00.

Country Kitchen Bijou Theatre Plate

Like the other advertising plates found on these 9½" plates, this one reads: "Compliments of Bijou Theatre." The lettering which is intaglio on the interior is very hard to see on a photo. $350.00.

Country Kitchen Castle Theatre Plate

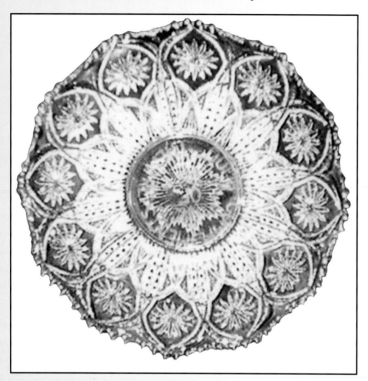

Still another of the Millersburg advertising plates in the 9½" size, this one says: "Compliments of the Castle Theatre." We haven't a clue as to where this theatre was but suspect it may have been Chicago. $350.00.

Country Kitchen Advertising Bowl

Several pieces in the Country Kitchen pattern are found with advertising in both bowls and plates. The bowls are about 8½" in diameter and most are ruffled. Here we show a rare ice cream bowl shape with the lettering: "COMPLIMENTS LOUIS MANKOWITZ — CLOAKS AND SUITS — #2 MILWAUKEE AVE — CHICAGO." There is also a ruffled bowl that says: "COMPLIMENTS OF ILLINOIS FURNITURE CO — HONEST VALUES — 3609 N. HALSTED ST." Of course *all* advertising pieces in Millersburg glass are scarce and very collectible and usually create a stir when listed in auction. $300.00.

Country Kitchen Berry Set (Ruffled)

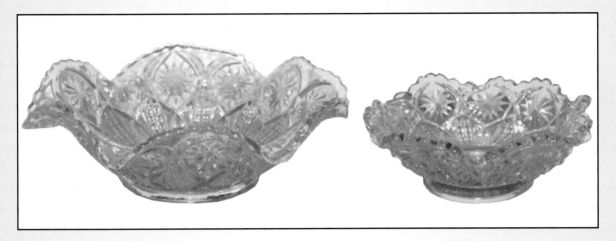

As opposed to the deep, round master bowl shown elsewhere, this berry set is ruffled. The large bowl measures about 8" across the top while the small bowl is 5¼". The larger bowl is often found but the small one is a bit hard to locate. Large, $90.00; small, $40.00.

Country Kitchen Opalescent Bowl

Look closely and you will see this is the *regular* Country Kitchen 7½" bowl with an opalescent treatment. It is the first of these we've heard about and just why all the others have been the variant (Milky Way) pattern is a mystery. Our thanks to Wally McDaniel and Richard Houghton for letting us show this rarity. $375.00, rare.

Country Kitchen Deep Round Bowl

This large bowl (8½" across and 4" deep) isn't often found by collectors. It is from the mould that produced the large size plate shape. The example shown has excellent clarity with good mould work throughout. We can imagine this bowl was also produced in a six-ruffle version but we only recall seeing the smaller berry bowls (8" x 3¼") with ruffling as well as the sauces. $100.00.

Country Kitchen Dome-based Bowl

Probably the rarest of all Country Kitchen bowls in crystal, this one has the dome base that is often seen in carnival glass with the Fleur-de-lis interior. It measures 10¼" across the top. The few I've seen are round as shown but carnival pieces are known in a rose bowl shape, ruffled, or tri-cornered, so we can't discount other shapings in crystal. $300.00, rare.

Country Kitchen Square Bowl

Shaped from the large berry bowl, this one has four sides pulled up to form a square. It measures about 9" on the diagonal and 6½" across. In the last few years we've encountered a number of whimsied shapes in this size bowl in this pattern. Others included a bowl with large ruffles that almost touch each other in their swing, the usual six-ruffled ones, ice cream shaped bowls, and even bowls that are just flared with no ruffling. $200.00, rare.

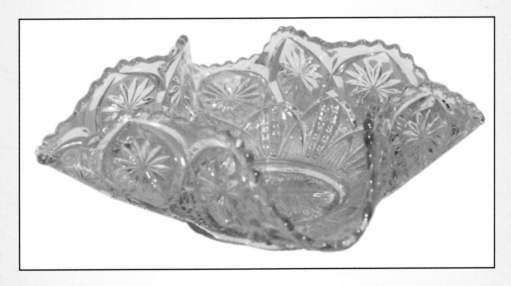

Country Kitchen Six-Pointed Whimsey Bowl

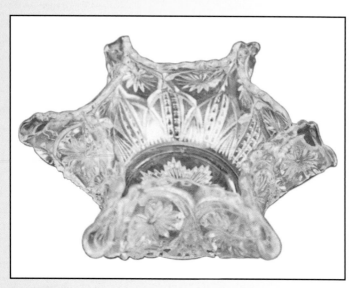

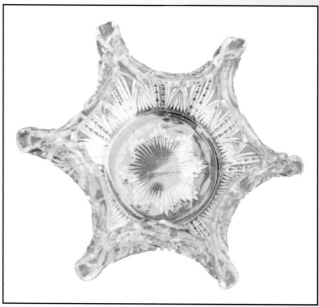

In all our travels looking at glass, we haven't seen a piece of glass that had been more whimsied than this Millersburg Country Kitchen bowl. Its sides have been curved in wide arcs that leave the six outer edges sticking out like scoops! And if that weren't enough, we've seen the same patterned bowl shaped in an opposite way with the arcs turned out and the points inward. Someone at the Millersburg factory certainly had a sense of humor. $325.00, rare. Thanks to Ben Hershberger for sharing this.

Country Kitchen Large and Small Rose Bowls

Found in 9" and 5" sizes, these rose bowl shapes are just the berry bowls that have been turned in around the top but they are much rarer and to show both sizes together is a real treat. The glass is clear and polished and each piece is a collector's prize. Large, $275.00; small, $150.00.

Country Kitchen 7" Rose Bowl

Besides the small rose bowl (from the sauce), and the larger 9" one from the master bowl, here is the 7" size that was shaped from the berry bowl size (large). Just why John Fenton made so many slightly different sizes in these bowls is a mystery, but we've seen at least three sizes in this pattern alone. $200.00, rare size.

Country Kitchen Variant Non-Opal Bowl

Here is the first example of the plain or non-opalescent bowl in the variant of the Country Kitchen or Milky Way bowl. It measures 9¼" across the top and is ice cream shaped. Certainly there are other sizes out there with no opalescent treatment so be aware of the possibility. $250.00, rare.

Country Kitchen Variant

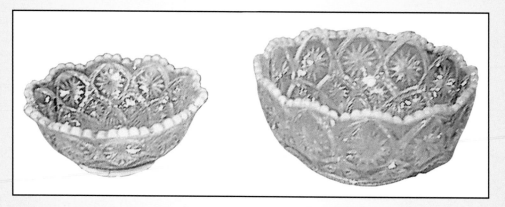

Shown are two round bowls, the smaller 5" one slightly flared and the larger 8" bowl deep with a straight top that stands almost straight up. This shape is very scarce indeed and appears almost as if it just came out of the mould. 5", $300.00; 8", $350.00.

Country Kitchen Variant (Large)

Just like the smaller size bowls in this pattern and treatment, but this one is a size larger and measures 7½" across. As you can see, this version is the six-ruffled shape but this larger version can also be found in a square shape or round one. We've been told the smaller bowls are a bit easier to find than these larger ones but actually both sizes are very scarce indeed. In addition, this larger bowl has twelve shield designs around it while the smaller version has only ten. $350.00.

Country Kitchen Variant (Small)

Called Milky Way by opalescent glass collectors, this variation of Millersburg's Country Kitchen pattern can be found in two sizes and various shapings. Shown is the small size in a square bowl, but it can be found in round shapes as well as a ruffled shape. The square one measures 4½" x 6". Few of these opalescent pieces are known and it seems (according to Frank M. Fenton) these were some of the experimental treatments John Fenton was trying near the end of the factory's life. There are ten shield shapes around this small bowl while the larger one has twelve. $350.00.

Country Kitchen Variant Large Square Bowl

Here is the 7½" square bowl in the opalescent variant pattern. Please note it has twelve of the fan-shields while the smaller version has only ten. In addition, the many rayed star on the bases of these variant pieces differs greatly from the star on the marie of regular Country Kitchen bowls, and matches the star on the marie of Millersburg River Glass Flute bowls shown elsewhere. $375.00.

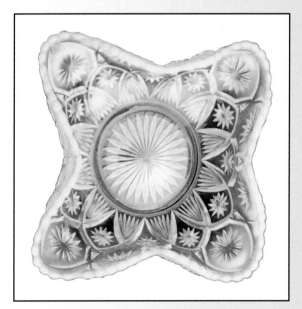

Country Kitchen Variant Gilded Square Bowl

Here is the Country Kitchen Variant bowl in the small size, just like the squared shape shown elsewhere but with gilded edges. It is the first of these opalescent bowls with this gilding we've seen but it adds a nice touch and probably more were finished in this way. One can only imagine what John Fenton may have produced if he had been able to stay in business a few years longer. $385.00.

Potpourri Deep Round Compote

This is different from the salver, the cake plate, and the goblet shapes, having a slightly flared top. It measures 7¼" across the top and is considered the standard shape in this piece. $100.00.

Potpourri Compote (Sapphire)

Like the crystal versions of this well-known deep bowled compote shape, except this one is sapphire blue. It is an ultra-rare item indeed. I think I've seen as many of these compotes in crystal as any other pattern or shape in crystal, still this is the only example of one in sapphire blue I've seen or even heard about. It is about 7¼" tall and has a top diameter of about 6½". $2,300.00, rare. Courtesy of Steve Maag.

Potpourri Whimsey Goblet

The piece shown here is the first of these we've been privileged to see and it is a unique item. Shaped just as it came out of the mould, the standard Potpourri compote has been left in this deep, straight shape we usually call a goblet shape. There are probably other examples of this shape but if so, they are well hidden and for now we feel this is rare and a desirable one-of-a-kind example of the glassmakers' art at Millersburg. $150.00.

Potpourri Salver

Here is a shape in this compote that seems a bit easier to find than any other. Now and then you can find one of these in antique malls where the price seems quite reasonable. It is the compote shape that has been flattened into what is known as a salver (a salver sat on an entry table for guests to put calling cards in when they were arriving at someone's home). These salvers, along with a deep, flared compote and a deep, straight compote, were advertised as a "High Footed Salver and Fruit Bowl Assortment," at 92 cents a dozen in Butler Brothers catalog. $75.00.

Potpourri Milk Pitcher

This 7" tall milk pitcher is found in rare marigold carnival glass where only two examples are reported and this equally rare crystal. The design is a spinoff of the Country Kitchen design with a daisy-wheel pattern added. The glass is clear and has a finished surface that gives it a sparkle. We suspect the number of these milk pitchers in crystal do not exceed a dozen but we could be wrong. At any rate, they always command attention and bring high prices when sold. $600.00, rare.

Potpourri Tumbler

This tumbler came as a real surprise when the photo arrived, since in the two decades since I last wrote about Millersburg crystal, I'd never heard of one of these. There are rare examples of the milk pitcher (shown elsewhere) but with the appearance of the tumbler shape, the possibility of a water pitcher seems less impossible. Anyone ever heard of one? $200.00, **very rare.** Courtesy of Wally McDaniel.

Flute or Wide Panel Variations

If anyone takes the time to examine the Millersburg Flute (or Wide Panel) exteriors, they are bound to find some differences; not only in the number of panels but in the base or marie designs (there are at least four). We suspect all this is because John Fenton had designs made for his production as well as bought moulds from others, such as the "Colonial" line of Ohio Flint Glass when they went out of business in 1907. It is for this reason we are showing under Flute some of the examples known to have been designed for the Millersburg factory and later we show a section called "river glass" that is shown in a 1910 Butler Brothers ad as a "world beater" colonial assortment. This assortment shows three sizes of bowls, a table set, water set, handled celery vase, a syrup, and an oil bottle. Folks we've talked to along the Ohio River near Cincinnati call this assortment "river glass" and say it was shipped down the river from eastern Ohio. It is interesting to note that the bowl's marie is the one found on the carnival glass pattern called Millersburg Grape.

And we'd like to call your attention to the maries in this section. The many rayed stars on the nappy, bonbon, and card tray are not like that found on the master ice cream bowl or the spooner, indicating our observations are indeed correct. In addition, the carnival "Courthouse" bowls have a third marie variation and the "river glass" pieces a fourth.

It all brings us to another Millersburg mystery and only enforces the fact that John Fenton did things his way, even if it can only cause us unending questions today.

Flute Bonbon

Similar to the nappy shown elsewhere, the bonbon shape is almost flat enough to be called a card tray. Few of these seem to be known and this is the second one we've seen. The quality of glass is typical of Millersburg crystal and is like a sparkling gem. $175.00, rare.

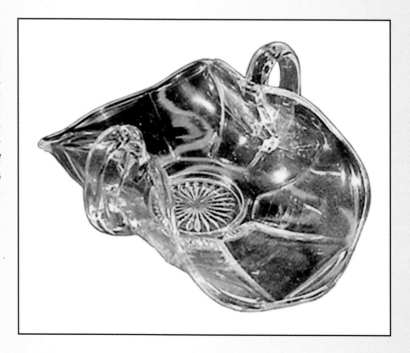

Flute Card Tray

Found as the exterior pattern on Holly Sprig, Night Stars, and Holly Whirl bonbons and card trays, the crystal Flute pieces are extremely rare. Here we show the card tray which is the bonbon flattened out. In addition, there is a Flute tri-cornered nappy in crystal. (I once owned it and sold it to Harold Wagner in 1997.) All the pieces in whatever shape are fine, clear glass with the usual Millersburg attention to quality. $175.00, rare.

Flute Nappy

Only a handful of these have been reported and I once owned one and was foolish enough to let it get away from me. All are roughly spade shaped (the example shown is more flared than spade shaped). Each piece is clear and sparkling. $200.00, rare.

Flute Master Ice Cream Bowl

Found in both berry sets with ruffled edges and this ice cream shaped bowl in both large and small sizes, this is the standard Millersburg Flute pattern. (As we said earlier, there is a second Flute or Wide Panel design that many Ohio collectors know as "river glass." It was the Flute pattern found on the exterior of Holly Sprig and Millersburg Grape bowls, and has a marie design of many rays rather than the star rays shown on this ice cream bowl.) $150.00.

Flute Jelly Compote (Ruffled)

This 6" compote, originally one of the moulds that came to Millersburg from the Ohio Flint Glass Company and still marked "crys-tal" (sic), is known in both marigold and amethyst carnival glass as well as in crystal. It was also used with the interior patterns of Wildflower or Acorn to add volume to the carnival line. Flute is rare in carnival glass and very scarce in crystal and is distinguished by its clover-leaf base design. $275.00.

Flute Unruffled Jelly Compote

The ruffled version of this 6" jelly compote was also used with the Wild Flower or the Acorn interiors in carnival glass. Most of these in crystal are six-ruffled but here we show a round one that is pretty much as it came from the mould. $300.00, rare shape.

Flute Round Compote (Large)

Here is the large Flute compote (some call it the Peacock blank compote) that isn't ruffled like most but is flared and round just as it came from the mould. They are rarer than the ruffled ones. $450.00, rare.

Flute Stemmed Cake Stand

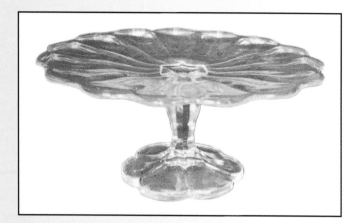

Here is the large clover-base compote that has been flattened on the top to produce a cake plate. This shape is extremely rare but is known on both the Flute and the Potpourri patterns, also pulled from the compote shape. In addition, at least one very rare example in this shape is known in the Hobstar and Feather pattern, pulled from the 6" compote shape. It is marigold carnival glass and is in Texas. $400.00, rare.

Large Flute Compote

Many collectors of Millersburg crystal do not realize this compote shape actually came in two sizes (7" or 8" tall) but it did and both sizes are listed in the Jefferson ads from their Canadian plant. Some call this the "Peacock Blank" compote because the carnival glass version of the 8" compote had the Peacock pattern on the interior. In any case, this, along with the 6" jelly compote in Flute, was purchased by John Fenton from the Ohio Flint Glass Colonial line when that plant closed. $350.00, either size.

Flute Milk Pitcher

This milk pitcher shape is just like the water set and the table set shown in a 1909 Butler Brothers catalog (there was also a syrup, a celery vase, an oil bottle, and several bowls). It is a very rare item indeed. On the same page are two other Millersburg ads, one showing Potpourri compotes and the other a crystal "Pacemaker" assortment. $150.00. Thanks to the Westons for sharing it.

Flute Punch Bowl

Shown in the ads from Jefferson's Canadian plant after the Millersburg plant closed, this bowl and base were apparently part of the Colonial line that Millersburg purchased from the Ohio Flint Glass factory after 1908. The example shown is marked CRYS-TAL (see insert) just like the clover-based jelly compote and the pieces of Venetian shown elsewhere. This punch bowl and stand was also used in carnival glass with the "Big Thistle" interior. Punch bowl and base, $625.00, rare; cup (if ever reported), $45.00 each.

Mark on the bottom of the punch bowl.

--- **Flute Hotel Sugar (Open)** ---

Millersburg actually had *two* Flute or Wide Panel lines and here is the most recognizable one. It includes the clover-base compotes (Peacock blank and Wildflower blank), the rare punch bowl and base, a bonbon, card tray, a spade-shaped nappy, and a berry set. The piece shown here is called a hotel sugar and is shown in a Jefferson Glass Company, Limited, Toronto, Canada catalog which featured glass patterns Jefferson had shipped to their Canadian plant after the purchase of the Millersburg factory. There is also a matching creamer. These patterns were Jefferson's #1600. $100.00, rare.

Hobstar and Feather

Believed to have been a pattern that was designed by John Fenton, this was one of the first two patterns advertised by the firm and was first produced in 1909 (mould drawings are indeed dated to this year in April, six weeks before glass was first produced).

Hobstar and Feather is distinguished by a typical hobstar with a button center (some pieces, especially those of the berry sets, have a prismatic center exactly like the Venetian pattern). Between the hobnails, deep cut feathers or leaves swirl in a languid style and the two designs seem to blend together for a pleasing but strong result. Hobstar and Feather can be found in plain or frosted treatment, ruby stain (rare), green stain (very rare), gilded (also rare), and occasionally allover frosting. Shapes are many and cover nearly every imaginable conformation.

The Millersburg Company called this the #358 pattern and early ads list it as a "sunburst and leaf" pattern. We believe this pattern was produced in some form of glass from the opening day to the last days of production at Millersburg and today, it remains one of their most collectible patterns, in both carnival glass and crystal. Note: Add 10% to the price listings for gilded pieces. Add 25% to price listings for frosted pieces.

Millersburg Ingenuity

Here are five shapes in Millersburg's 6" jelly compote in the Hobstar and Feather pattern. These include the standard flared version, the ruffled compote, the shallow ice cream shaped compote, the rose bowl whimsey, and the banana bowl whimsey. All this shows the unique ways a company can stretch one pattern and shape into many, thus working their magic for additional sales.

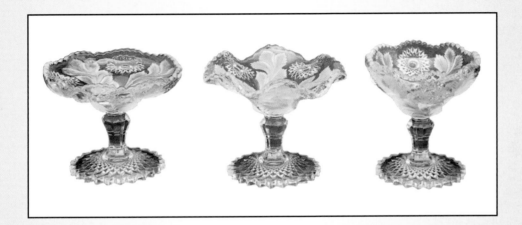

Hobstar and Feather Small Banana Boat (Frosted)

Just like the smaller example shown elsewhere in a plain finish, except this one is frosted and matches the frosted large boats. The example shown measures 6" x 4½" and is from the same mould as the hand-grip plate, the diamond-shaped plate, and the nut bowls. $300.00.

Hobstar and Feather Banana Bowls

Here we show both the large bowl (11½" long, 8" wide, and 4" deep) and the matching small bowl (6" long, 4½" wide, and 2½" deep). Both sizes are found in either plain or frosted glass and while the larger size is a bit more plentiful than the small size, we'd guess they were originally meant to make up a table set with one large bowl and six small ones. Do not confuse these pieces with the shallower and smaller celery boat shown elsewhere. They are from two entirely different moulds. Large, $75.00; small, $60.00.

Hobstar and Feather Tri-Cornered Small Bowl

Shaped from the small sauce bowl, this little jewel can be found either plain or frosted. It measures about 5¼" across and has three corners turned in while the remaining three sides are flattened out to give it a very graceful shape. These whimsey pieces are quite rare and a favorite of collectors. They are a perfect match to the Ohio Star tri-cornered bowls shown elsewhere in this book. $250.00.

Hobstar and Feather Deep Master Bowl

When you look at this bowl from the top, it looks almost square but it isn't. It measures 8" across and is almost 4" deep. The example shown was purchased in the Millersburg area and is frosted but we are certain non-frosted examples exist. Had the top been turned in a bit more, we would have had a large flat rose bowl but this shape is just as rare. $250.00.

Hobstar and Feather Ice Cream Bowls

Found on both large and small bowls that are rather shallow and have the edges turned up, these so-called ice cream sets probably never were used to hold ice cream but were more than likely salad bowls. The large bowl measures about 9½" across and the smaller one is around 5". We've seen these bowls in both plain or frosted varieties and a complete set is a treasure. Large, $75.00; small, $35.00.

Hobstar and Feather Sauce with Maiden Blush

We know of about four or five of these small sauce bowls that have this treatment of cranberry staining called Maiden Blush. The example shown also has most of the original gilding on the top edges. The staining is very clear and watery, often hard to see unless it is held in the proper lighting, but is definitely there. Please note that the center of the hobnails are prismatic just like all the other berry set pieces. We haven't seen these sauce bowls ruffled in this treatment but they probably exist. $150.00.

Hobstar and Feather Banana Bowl Whimsey

Pulled from the large ice cream bowl, this stretched out version with two sides pulled up and rolled in measures about 11" long. Found mostly in plain crystal, a few of these have been reported in frosted glass. A rare shape despite its irregular design. $350.00.

Hobstar and Feather Small Applesauce

Found in both frosted and plain pieces this applesauce bowl has been turned up slightly on the long edges and pulled in tightly on the narrow sides. These bowls are generally about 4" wide and have a length of approximately 8". The centers of the Hobstars are button shaped rather than prismatic so we know they were not shaped from the berry set pieces. These bowls should be classified as very scarce rather than rare as they show up rather frequently compared to most Millersburg crystal. Small, $150.00.

Hobstar and Feather Large Applesauce

Larger than the other example of this dish but shaped the same (this one is 10½" long), with two sides turned in and the opposite ends flattened. Note that this example is also frosted but we've seen it both ways. Large, $175.00.

Hobstar and Feather Green Stain/Gilded Sauce

We understand there are at least two or three of these known with this treatment and all seem to be found in the sauce bowl shape. The feathers are stained (unlike the ruby stained pieces where the backgrounds have the staining), and the edges are gilded. $250.00, rare. Thanks to the Houghtons for sharing this rare item.

Hobstar and Feather Celery Boat

This piece is deeper than the pickle or relish trays, and somewhat shallower than the banana bowls, and not often seen. It measures roughly 10" in length and has a width of about 5". The feathers can be either frosted or plain but frosted examples are scarcer. The glass on this piece is very thick, heavy, and clear, making it quite desirable, but like many of the sawtoothed-edged bowls, the teeth are often damaged and to find a perfect example is difficult. $175.00.

Hobstar and Feather Large Square Bowl

Here is a real showstopper. It is the large bowl that measures 11" across and was pulled from the large ice cream bowl shape into this square whimsey. As you can see, the feathers are frosted as are the three or four of these we've heard about. The button center of the hobstars are prismatic. $250.00.

Hobstar and Feather Fully Frosted Bowl

Here is the only example we've seen of this piece but others probably exist. This is the large ice cream bowl that has been completely frosted on the exterior giving it a satiny look. It is in Millersburg and we were privileged to handle it in 1999. $350.00.
Thanks to the Elliot Sheelys.

Hobstar and Feather Medium Square Bowl

Like the larger version and the 6" version, this medium size bowl (8" x 8") has the corners turned up to form the square. Like most of the others, this one is frosted. $250.00.

Hobstar and Feather Nut Bowl Whimsey

Similar to the mint bowl shown elsewhere, this nut bowl measures 5⅞" x 4¼" and is just a bit smaller than the former. In addition the crimping is more subtle and not turned up as much. It has been reported in both clear and frosted examples. $300.00.

Hobstar and Feather Small Gilded Rose Bowl

This small rose bowl was shaped from the ice cream bowl and measures 4½" across. It is frosted and has gilding on the top sawtooth edging. We now believe many more items were gilded than we've thought. $220.00.

Hobstar and Feather Covered Butter Dish

When you see both the Ohio Star and the Hobstar and Feather butter dishes, it is difficult to decide which is more beautiful. Both are on clear, polished glass and both show the design to perfection. The Hobstar and Feather pieces can be found both plain or frosted. $275.00.

Hobstar and Feather Creamer

About the same size as the Ohio Star table set pieces, the Hobstar and Feather examples have dimpled handles rather than notched and the glass seems a bit thinner. Pieces in this set are considered rare too and just as desirable. $100.00.

Hobstar and Feather Covered Sugar

Matching the other shapes in this table set, this piece has a bit heavier look and the lid's finial adds to this perception. Again, the piece may be found clear or frosted and all pieces are clear and well polished. $150.00.

Hobstar and Feather Covered Sugar (Ruby Stain)

Here is the only reported example of this shape in the ruby stain treatment, and like the five other reported pieces (all shapes), it is rare and very desirable. We'd certainly like to hear from anyone owning additional shapes in this treatment. $600.00. Thanks to the Lickvers for sharing this piece.

Hobstar and Feather Spooner

This spooner, found with two handles that are dimpled to match the rest of the serving items in this pattern, may be plain glass or have frosted feathers. The shape of the spooner, creamer, or covered sugar is the one that rolls out at the middle and is not a squat look. $100.00.

Hobstar and Feather Spooner (Ruby Stain)

What a privilege to show another piece of this very rare ruby stain treatment. All known pieces from Millersburg are Hobstar and Feather and include a nut bowl, two spooners, a spade bridge piece, a club bridge piece, and a covered sugar. $550.00, rare.

Hobstar and Feather Handled Basket

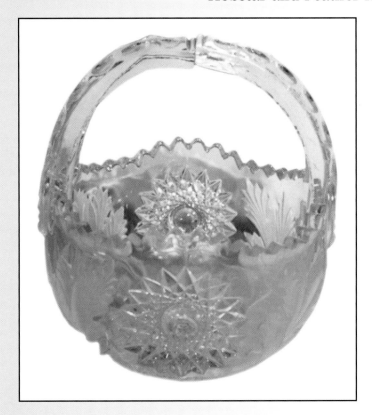

For years only one of these rare handled baskets was known, but in the last few years, more examples have come forward and now we know of seven examples. All except two are frosted, stand 5" tall and measure 5" across. The handles are moulded at the sides and were originally two blades when removed from the mould. They were then bent while the glass was pliable to meet in the center and on most examples just touch rather than join together. Another Millersburg rarity that is uniquely designed. The handles have the same inverted dots found on the Hobstar and Feather water pitcher handle and the pieces were apparently designed to match. $900.00, rare.

Hobstar and Feather Plain Basket

Unlike the frosted example shown previously, this one has no frosting and is a bit harder to find. We currently know of seven of these baskets and only two are non-frosted, but there are certainly more out there. $900.00.

Hobstar and Feather Jelly Compote (Unfrosted)

Just like the frosted example we show below, here is the unfrosted jelly compote which is much easier to find. Both measure 6" tall and the design just seems to fit this shape to perfection. In addition, both clear and frosted compotes can be found ruffled. These are rarer and always bring a higher price when sold. Flared, $100.00; ruffled, $250.00.

Hobstar and Feather Jelly Compote (Frosted)

Known in rare carnival items (a compote, footed card tray whimsey), this staple of the crystal line is still a great item for Millersburg collectors. It is usually found as shown in a flared compote shape but can also be seen in a few whimsey shapes that include a rose bowl shape, flattened ice cream bowl shape, a banana stand whimsey, and a flat card tray. In addition, there is at least one example in crystal that has the feathers gilded. The jelly compote can be found in either plain or frosted treatments. It stands roughly 5½" tall and stands on a paneled stem and elaborately faceted base that has a hobstar. Flared, $110.00; ruffled, $350.00.

Hobstar and Feather Stemmed Rose Bowl Whimsey (Unfrosted)

Made from the 6" compote mould, most of these whimsey rose bowls have frosted feathers but this example is clear. It is actually the first non-frosted example we've seen so we felt it was well worth showing. $225.00.

Hobstar and Feather Stemmed Rose Bowl Whimsey (Frosted)

Pulled from the 6" jelly compote shape, this stemmed rose bowl whimsey is one of the jewels in this pattern. It can be found in clear or frosted glass, but most of the ones I've seen are frosted. In availability, these rose bowl whimsies are a bit easier to find than others from Millersburg, but I would still classify this piece as rare and don't expect to run into one of these very often. They are desirable and very collectible. $275.00.

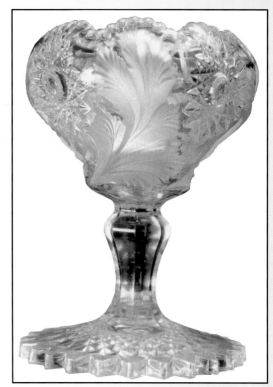

Hobstar and Feather Gilded Jelly Compote

Unlike most of the 6" compotes in this pattern, this one has gilding on the feathers and along the top's serrated edges, making it a bit different. I have no idea just how many of these are out there, but this is the first I've seen. We did know Millersburg did some gilding on this pattern since the bowl with Maiden Blush (cranberry) stain has this gilding. $125.00.

Hobstar and Feather Banana Stand Whimsey

We've heard of three of these rare whimsies but more probably exist. It was pulled from the standard 6" stemmed compote, then rolled and shaped like a banana stand. All examples we've heard about are frosted but non-frosted examples probably exist. And imagine our surprise when we spotted one of these in a display window at the 1999 Millersburg Fall Festival among a huge assortment of other Millersburg crystal rarities. $350.00, rare.

Hobstar and Feather Card Tray Whimsey

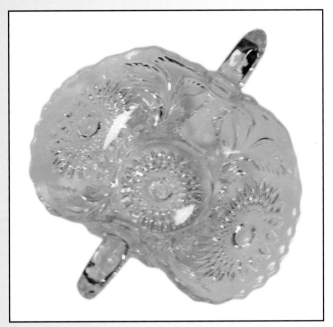

Here is a rarity many Millersburg collectors haven't seen or even heard about. We hadn't until we saw it in Millersburg in 1999. It is a whimsied two-handled card tray, pulled from the spooner shape. What a treasure it has to be for its lucky owner and I only wish there were more of these around so I could claim one. It measures roughly 7½" x 8" and is on clear glass. $350.00, rare. Thanks to Wes Schmucker for sharing it.

Hobstar and Feather Cracker Jar (Clear)

Sometimes called a cookie jar, this was the first piece of Millersburg crystal advertised in Butler Brothers catalogs in 1909. Massive, with two handles and a matching lid, the piece is very impressive, and isn't easy to find today. We've heard of clear and frosted examples and both are considered rare. $500.00.

Hobstar and Feather Cracker Jar (Frosted)

Here's the frosted version of this massive, two-handled cracker or cookie jar with lid. It is a bit harder to find than the clear version shown on page 75 but both are considered rare and desirable. $600.00.

Hobstar and Feather Mint Dish

Often called a nut dish but probably used for other things, this piece is just like the ruby stain dish shown on page 77. It measures 5" x 6" with four sides turned up. It can be found plain or frosted as well as stained and is rare in all treatments. The example shown was recently sold as a square plate at the price listed but it isn't a plate as anyone can plainly see. $350.00.

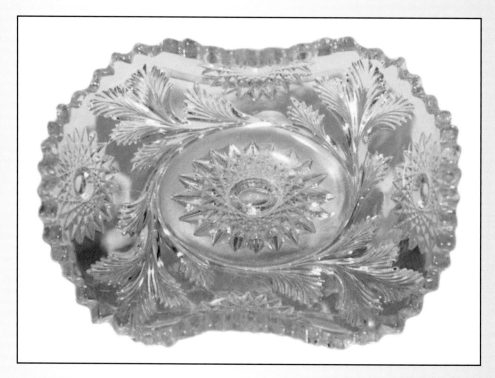

Hobstar and Feather Mint Dish (Ruby Stain)

What a joy it is to finally show this very rare Hobstar and Feather mint or nut dish. It measures 5" x 6" and is rolled up on four sides. It is the only reported example with a ruby stain treatment (a covered sugar, spooner, a club piece from the bridge set are also known in this treatment). And when my co-author called to tell me it was in a sale and he would bid for me, I slept very little until he called again to say it was on its way to me. It is the crown jewel of my collection and I count my blessings every time I look at it. $600.00, rare.

Hobstar and Feather Mammoth Pitcher (clear with plain base)

Here is the non-frosted version of this super pitcher with a plain base. This one stands 8¼" tall as compared to the frosted one shown elsewhere that was somewhat shorter and had a more pronounced pulled-in neck. We believe these shape and height differences were due to the handler's work but can't explain why some of these pitchers are found with a rayed base. $1,000.00.

Hobstar and Feather Frosted Mammoth Pitcher

What a joy it is to show this frosted version of a rare, rare pitcher. For years we'd heard rumors that a frosted example was known but we hadn't seen it until we got this photo from Richard Houghton. This pitcher has a plain base and stands 7⅞" tall. $1,200.00.

Hobstar and Feather Mammoth Pitcher (clear with rayed base)

The only word to describe this rare and desirable pitcher is impressive. It was first advertised in Butler Brothers catalog in October 1909, and sold for 35 cents each! It stands 8" tall, has a girth of 22½", and holds 3½" quarts of liquid. But to describe it as anything besides one of the rarities of Millersburg crystal would be to slight a real treasure. Even damaged examples sell for high prices when they are found and a search for one of these pitchers may take years. (Eighteen years in my case, but it was worth the wait!) This pitcher has the many rayed star base. $1,000.00, rare.

Hobstar and Feather Spoutless Tankard Pitcher (Frosted)

Here is what the famous Hobstar and Feather tankard water pitcher looks like as prepared for the added metal top, shown elsewhere. It is just as it came from the mould without a pouring lip. The example shown is frosted but it is known in non-frosted finish also. This one belongs to Norm Archer and is one of three spoutless examples I've heard about. It is a real rarity and a unique and desirable item. $850.00, rare.

Hobstar and Feather Metal Top Pitchers

These tankard pitchers with the applied metal tops are so rare that few collectors have been privileged to see one. There are two designs of metal work, one with a shallow rim that is beaded with a flower band, and one with a wide rim that has a different design of teardrops and scrollwork. We have no idea if these tops were put on at the Millersburg plant or farmed out but we also will show a pitcher with no spot that was meant to receive a metal top and didn't. We estimate there are five to nine of these pitchers known throughout the United States and four of those known are frosted. $1,250.00, rare.

Hobstar and Feather Tumbler

The undulating shape of this tumbler is a special feature and with the strong added design, it becomes one of the better tumbler designs in all of crystal. The top flares just enough to add to the overall appearance too. A really great tumbler! $75.00 each.

Hobstar and Feather Pickle Dishes

Shown are two of three sizes in this shape (sizes are 7½" long, 8½" long, and 10" long). In addition, we have heard of an even larger example but haven't seen it. It is roughly diamond shaped and the edges turn up evenly all the way around. Examples in both clear and frosted are known. 7½", $40.00; 8½", $60.00; 10", $75.00.

Hobstar and Feather Sapphire Pickle Dish

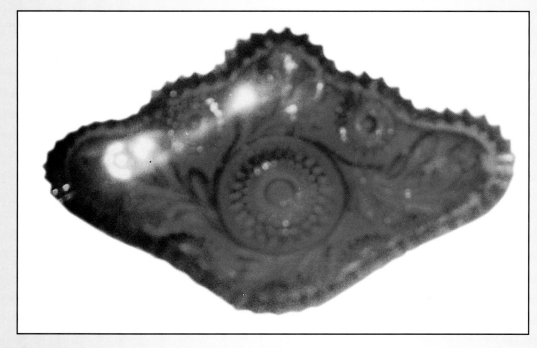

Only a handful of Millersburg pieces are known in sapphire blue crystal and here is one of the least known. For years this piece rested in the collection of the late Dorothy Close (right beside the two opalescent Ohio Star vases), and I was promised this piece would one day be mine. Unfortunately, that day hasn't come (I'm still hoping). It is a standard pickle or relish dish and measures 7" long. I feel confident there are probably other pieces of this pattern in colored crystal but none are known at this time. $1,200.00 rare.

Hobstar and Feather Diamond Tray (Medium)

This flat frosted tray measures 8" x 12" and was made from the small oval boat shape we show elsewhere. It matches the large (11½" x 14½") one shown elsewhere, and there is also a smaller version that is roughly 5" x 8". Most seen are frosted. $300.00.

Hobstar and Feather Handgrip Plate

This rarity is found on three reported examples, but there may be more in various glass collections. The known pieces are all frosted. This piece may be made from the small banana bowl mould. It measures 8" in length and has a width of 5½". It sits nearly flat and has a ground base. Incidentally, the ruby stained mint dish was also pulled from this same mould. $500.00.

Hobstar and Feather Small Round Plate

Here is the smallest of the round plates in this pattern and we can verify besides this 5" example, there are others in 7", 9", and 11" sizes as well. All sizes seem to have been made in mostly frosted examples but a few of the smaller sizes are known in clear as well. 5", $100.00; 7", $150.00; 9", $250.00; 11" – 12", $500.00.

Hobstar and Feather Large Round Plate

On close examination, this plate isn't truly round but has four points (one at the end of each feathered section), but most collectors call this the large round plate. As you can see it is frosted as are most in this size but we have heard of at least one non-frosted example. It measures 11¾" in diameter. $600.00.

Hobstar and Feather Platter

This very rare platter (11½" x 14½") was shaped from the large banana bowl and as far as we know is the first of this size and shape to be reported. (There is a smaller 7½" x 5½" one made from the small banana bowl.) This piece has frosted feathers and is a standout in size and finish, and would be the crowning piece in any Millersburg collection. We now believe there are at least two more of these so at least three must exist. $750.00.

Hobstar and Feather Punch Set

Found in both carnival glass and crystal, this massive punch set is a treasure. It can be found either clear or frosted (frosted sets are rarer) and it would be hard to choose between this set and the Ohio Star as to beauty. Both are thick, sparkling glass with deep cut designs that are flawless. Shapes in crystal for the punch bowl tops are flared, goblet shaped (very rare), and tulip shaped (very rare). Cup, plain, $35.00; cup, frosted, $40.00; bowl and base, flared, plain, $1,200.00; bowl and base, flared, frosted, $1,400.00; goblet shape, plain, $1,350.00; goblet shape, frosted, $1,450.00; tulip top, plain, $1,450.00; tulip top, frosted, $1,600.00.

Hobstar and Feather Punch Set (Frosted)

Here is the frosted version of this massive punch set with the bowl's top slightly flared. It is a bit harder to find than the clear set and brings more money when sold but either treatment is a real find. Bowl and base, $1,400.00; cups, $40.00 each.

Hobstar and Feather Goblet-shaped Punch Bowl

Unlike most of these sets which have bowls that are flared at the top, this one is goblet-shaped with a slight ruffling at the very top. It is clear crystal and seems to be a bit more shallow than most sets. **Bowl and base, $1,450.00.** Thanks to Wally McDaniel for this truly rare item.

Hobstar and Feather Flat Rose Bowl

Shown is the flat-based small rose bowl, shaped from a sauce, but the larger berry bowl is also known to have been whimsied into this shape. One collector in Millersburg is said to have a complete set of these pieces. Most are frosted, but some have been found that are not. All are rare and costly and are quickly snatched up when they come up for sale. $200.00.

Hobstar and Feather Large Rose Bowl

Shaped from the berry bowl, this large rose bowl is 9" across and has frosted feathers, but it can be found without the frosting as well. We also show the 5½" example of this shape elsewhere. $275.00.

Hobstar and Feather Stemmed Sherbet

We've now seen this little gem in a flared shape, a ruffled shape, a straight-topped shape, and turned in like a rose bowl. All shapes are very popular with collectors. Both plain and frosted examples exist and the base has eight scallops. The flared example is about 4" tall with a nearly 4" bowl diameter. Years ago these sherbets were pretty much overlooked by collectors and brought small prices, but on today's market this is certainly not the case, and you can expect to pay a real price for them. Flared, $75.00; goblet, $100.00; rose bowl, $150.00; ruffled, $150.00.

Hobstar and Feather Giant Compote Whimsey

Pulled from the fabulous giant rose bowl shape, this rare and outstanding compote shape (some collectors call this a one-piece punch bowl whimsey) is at the top of the collectible field. There are two examples reported in carnival glass (one green and one amethyst) and this single example in crystal. I filmed this piece in a Festival display window in 1981, never dreaming that I would one day own it — now it is prominent in my collection. $2,000.00, rare.

Hobstar and Feather Metal Based Compote Whimsey

This is the first of these we've seen and it certainly is a standout piece of glass. The ice cream shaped bowl has been fused to a metal stand or base, giving it the look of a beautiful compote. The feathers are frosted on this piece but it may have been made without the frosting too. Surely there are more of these out there but if so, we haven't seen them. It measures 5½" across and was found in England. $250.00, rare.
Thanks to the Norman Archers for this beauty.

Hobstar and Feather Giant Rose Bowl

If I could own only one piece of Millersburg glass, this would be it, hands down. For its size (9" tall), it is the most impressive piece of glass around, bar none. Found in carnival glass as well as crystal, this giant rose bowl shape can also be found in whimsied pieces that include a flared compote shape and a flattened ice cream shape, both shown in this book. Pieces can be either clear or frosted. The whimsies are all clear and only one of the compote shapes in crystal and two in carnival glass are known, while the flattened or ice cream shape isn't reported in carnival glass and two or three are known in crystal. The glass is thick and massive and the design really stands out proudly. $1,500.00.

Hobstar and Feather Giant Ice Cream Stemmed Whimsey

When I had the chance to add this shape to my collection I jumped at it, for I love the pattern and the shape was unique. There are at least two of these known (and possibly more) and in 1999 we saw one in the Millersburg area. The piece has been pulled from the giant rose bowl and then flared and flattened into a bowl shape. No examples of this shape are reported in carnival glass so far but I wouldn't be surprised if one turned up. $2,000.00, rare.

Hobstar and Feather Giant Shallow Ice Cream Whimsey

Just like the example shown above except this is much shallower and really identifies with the ice cream shaping. These are the only two of this shaping so far reported. It is 9½" wide and stands 7" tall. $2,000.00, rare. Courtesy of Ben Hershberger.

Hobstar and Feather Bridge Set

Occasionally you can find a single piece of this bridge set (they were advertised in Butler Brothers catalog as "bonbon dishes" at 39 cents a dozen), but to find a complete set is very rare indeed. They are known in both plain crystal or frosted crystal, but one rare example of the club piece is shown in the Fenton Museum in ruby stain. The first ads for this set appeared in October 1909, and the pieces were still advertised as late as spring 1912, indicating they must have sold well; but if that is true, where are they today? $75.00 each piece.

Hobstar and Feather Club Piece (Ruby Stain)

Here is the second piece of the bridge set to be reported in ruby stain (it is in the Fenton Museum). The diamond and heart shapes haven't been reported to date. All pieces of this pattern with ruby staining are very rare and desirable. $550.00, rare. We certainly thank Harold and Sherry Smith for sharing this rare item with us.

Hobstar and Feather Spittoon Whimsey

Fashioned from the tumbler shape, this piece is rare indeed. The feathers are not frosted and the hobstar's center button is plain rather than prismatic. It measures 2⅞" tall and has a top diameter of 3½". $3,000.00. Thanks to Mark Boley for sharing this piece.

Hobstar and Feather Water Set (Frosted)

Called a tankard water set by collectors, this pitcher and tumbler can be found in either clear or frosted examples. The pitcher is 9¼" tall and has a moulded handle that is patterned with inverted thumbprints. The matching tumblers are about 3¾" tall and are belled with the design ending about an inch from the top. Rare pitchers exist without a pouring lip or with a decorative metal top added but these are oddities that are seldom seen. Pitcher, $450.00; tumbler, $75.00 each.

Hobstar and Feather Pitcher (Clear)

Unlike the frosted example shown elsewhere, this one has the feathers unfrosted, giving the pitcher a softer look. We've seen more frosted examples than the clear, so despite the former being more desired and selling for more, we believe the non-frosted are really scarcer. $400.00.

Ohio Star

Designated Millersburg's #353 pattern and made from that first day (along with Hobstar and Feather), this fantastic design is also credited to John Fenton and the mould drawings are dated April 1909.

Ohio Star is recognized by the six-pointed star (the water bottle has eight points to fit the allowed space) that is rayed, paired with a geometric oval that has two inner ovals of file and two starbursts at the top and bottom of these file sections. The mould is deeply cut in and the glass is heavy, sparkling clear, and highly polished, giving each piece a finished look.

There are nearly as many shapes in Ohio Star as there are in Hobstar and Feather in crystal, and only a giant or massive compote seems to have been overlooked. In carnival glass only the vase shape and its whimsies, a tall jelly compote, a rare short compote, and a tri-cornered bowl whimsey are reported at this time, but in crystal the pattern really comes into its own with over two dozen shapes known.

Ohio Star Card Tray Whimsey

Here's a novelty piece that is a super find. It is 4¼" long and 3½" wide, rolling slightly upward from the base. In addition, a larger size with the same shape is reported that measures about 9½" in length. $150.00.

Ohio Star Compote (Short)

Here is the short compote in crystal, just like the sapphire blue one shown below. It stands 4¾" tall and measures 5¼" across the top. The glass is quite thick and clear with all the polished quality Millersburg gave this pattern. The serrated base has a huge Ohio Star design that matches the rest of the piece, and adds to the look. $125.00.

Ohio Star Compote (Sapphire Blue)

What a beauty this rare compote is. We've heard of only two examples but certainly others may exist. It was first shown in Marie McGee's book and has been with one or two Millersburg displays at conventions. We first got to see it in 1999 at the Millersburg Festival and it lives up to its billing. The coloring is a very rich sapphire and the glass is sparkling. The Ohio Star sapphire blue compote joins the ranks of the Hobstar and Feather sapphire blue pickle dish and the sapphire blue Potpourri compote in beauty and rarity. $1,650.00, very rare. Thanks to Steve Maag.

Ohio Star Tall Cupped Jelly Compote

Here is the second shaping of this 9" jelly compote on a tall stem. Its bowl is deeper and cupped up rather than the salver shape shown elsewhere. In addition, there is a third top shape that is like an ice cream bowl shape. $325.00.

Ohio Star Deep Cupped Jelly Compote

Like the shallow cupped example shown elsewhere, but this one is much deeper and stands 9½" tall. The bowl is almost goblet shaped and is one of the prettier shapes we've seen in this piece. $325.00.

Ohio Star Tall Jelly Compote (Salver)

The tall jelly compote on a solid glass square stem is about 7½" tall. It can be found with the top cupped up, giving it a deeper look, or like the one shown that is shallower and often has a ruffled edge. The glass is very thick on these pieces and crystal clear, making them very desirable and very rare. These compotes are also known in marigold carnival glass where they are even rare. $325.00.

Ohio Star Cruet

Cruets seem to have a fascination all their own and some collectors buy and treasure nothing else. If this is your situation, the Ohio Star cruet has to be high on your list. It is nearly 6" tall and has a large belled body with a flared neck and notched handle. The stopper that originally came with the cruets (most seen are not original) also has a star design that seems to wrap around it from the top down. I've only seen one of these stoppers and it looks just right when in place. As usual, the glass is thick, sparkling, and well polished. A real treasure that is rare but sometimes available. $225.00.

Ohio Star Shakers

This is one of the rarest shapes in this pattern, so a pair of them would be a real standout in any collection. In 30 years, less than 10 sets have been reported to us, but certainly more may exist. They are heavy glass, very polished, and look like teardrops in shape. Occasionally a shaker will be slightly taller than its mate, but that isn't a problem because of the rare status they hold. $450.00 each.

Ohio Star Water Bottle

Sometimes called a carafe, this water bottle is a large and heavy piece of glass that has been finished nicely with a flared top and a spoke-and-notch design on the neck. It stands nearly 9" tall and the most unusual aspect is the large star which has eight spokes rather than the usual six. This was done to fill the elongated space on the body of the bottle and has caused some collectors to doubt this piece is really Ohio Star, but the rest of the design is identical to Ohio Star and the quality of the glass leaves no doubt of its origin. $250.00.

Ohio Star 10" Celery Bowl (or Tray)

Shaped just like the pickle bowl shown elsewhere, this is the 10" celery bowl shape, but there is also a 9" one in the same shape too. This piece is pulled from the large ice cream bowl and the example here measures 10" x 6½". $225.00.

Ohio Star Cider Pitcher

While this tankard pitcher looks rather massive, it is deceptive and is really only 10" tall. Like the Ohio Star vase, it bells at both the top and the base and is of very heavy glass. The pitcher has a matching tumbler that is also belled and stands about ½" taller than the regular tumbler in this pattern. The pouring spout on the pitcher is hand shaped (like that on the Hobstar and Feather pitcher) and the base shows a stem of glass from the punty rod. The cider pitcher is easier to find than the standard Ohio Star pitcher and sells for much less, but it is still a very collectible item that has a real appeal to collectors. $200.00.

Ohio Star Flat Mint Dish (Gilded)

Shown in a 1910 ad, this Ohio Star mint dish measures 5¼" across and was the small flat plate shape that had been turned up slightly on all four sides. It is usually found on plain crystal but here we are happy to show a rare gilded example, indicating it came along later in Millersburg's production. Incidentally the ad listed these novelty mint dishes at 3½ cents each! $160.00.

Ohio Star Ice Cream Bowls

Just as in the Hobstar and Feather sets, these ice cream bowls in the Ohio Star pattern are round, shallow, and have the edges turned up. These sets are harder to find than their companion pattern and the large size bowls are very hard to find. The pattern shows well on this shape however and a complete set is almost a rarity. $100.00, large; $50.00, small.

Ohio Star Master Berry Bowl

Here is the deep master berry bowl in the Ohio Star pattern. It measures 8½" across and is a real beauty. Do not confuse this with the ice cream bowl which is more shallow. $150.00.

Ohio Star Small Berry Bowl

This small bowl matches the master berry bowl shown above and measures 4½" across. It is harder to find than the small ice cream bowls which are not as deep and not as flared. $60.00.

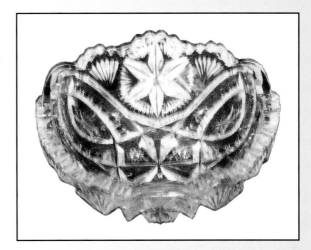

Ohio Star Medium Deep Bowl

Not only is this 6¼" bowl an odd size, but the design in the base is different from both the master or the small berry bowls. Just why this size was made is a mystery but here it is. $125.00, rare.

Ohio Star Pickle Bowl

This oval bowl with the sides turned up is like the celery bowl shown elsewhere in shape but measures only 7½" long. We are a bit puzzled as to just what bowl it was shaped from, but it may have been one of the square bowls that ended in this configuration. $150.00.

Ohio Star Plates

While this probably isn't a complete listing of sizes, we've seen Ohio Star plates in 5", 7", 9", and 11" sizes. Every one is round in shape and very rare. The small size is pulled from the sauce dish while the two larger sizes are pulled from bowls. The 7" size has always been a mystery as to just what mould was used but I'm guessing it was the same as the 5¼" squared mint dish. 5", $100.00; 7", $150.00; 9", $200.00; 11", $350.00.

Ohio Star Punch Set

Rare, immense, and spectacular are all words that are fitting to describe this wonderful punch set with its thick glass and deep-cut look that only Millersburg achieved on such crystal-clear glass. We suspect less than 20 of these complete sets exist and whenever one is offered for sale, the price just climbs over the previous sale. Larger than the Hobstar and Feather set (which is certainly massive in its own right), the Ohio Star punch set is a gem for collectors. Bowl and base, $1,400.00; cup, $35.00 each.

Ohio Star Punch Cup Whimsey

This has to be one of the neatest little whimsies we've run across. It is made from the punch cup and has been flattened out to a plate shape with the handle in a normal position. Only the one example has been reported and it has to be a real treasure for the owner. **$1,000.00.** Thanks to Steve Hall for sharing this rarity.

Ohio Star Rose Bowls

We're very happy to be able to show both the large and small size flat rose bowls, pulled from the berry set pieces. To find one of these is a real experience but to see them both together is remarkable. In all the 30 years I've been collecting Millersburg crystal, I've never seen a bad piece of Ohio Star; there probably are some but I haven't seen them. The glass is always clear, shining, and beautiful. The large bowl is about 7¼" across and the small bowl measures 4¼" diameter. Large, $350.00; small, $225.00.

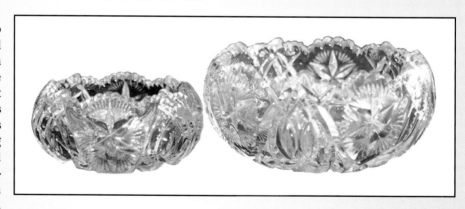

Ohio Star Square Bowl (Small)

This small square bowl (6" x 6") is very different from the square dish or the square mint dish. Both of the latter were square when they came from the mould while this example was round and had the four sides pulled in and the other four sides pulled down, giving it a square look. $100.00.

Ohio Star Square Bowl (Large)

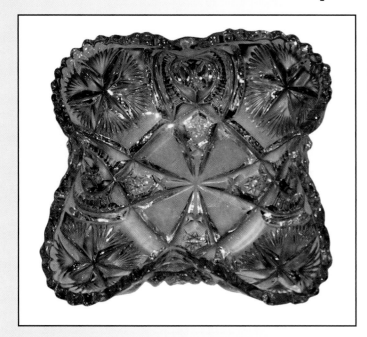

This deep, squared bowl is a different size than most we've seen, measuring 8½" across from corner to corner. Please note that the under pattern comes into the center like a cross with no center base design. $150.00. Thanks to the Lickvers for this piece.

Ohio Star 10" Ruffled Square Bowl

Similar to the 6" square bowl shown elsewhere, this one measures 10" across and has six ruffles, while the former has only four ruffles. A close look reveals this is a very gracefully shaped bowl and certainly not easily found. $150.00.

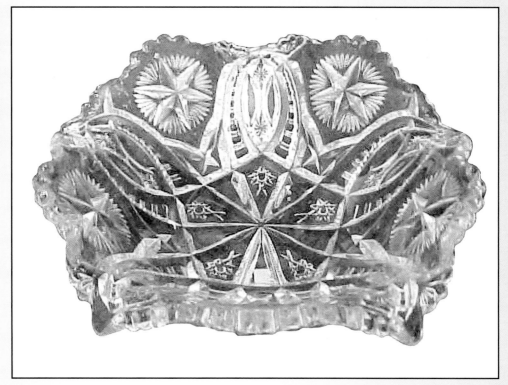

Ohio Star Square Dish

Slightly deeper than the square bowls, this piece is found in 5", 7", and 9" sizes. The dish has four Ohio Stars on opposing sides and four geometric ovals in the corners. It is pretty much shaped as it came out of the mould except for flaring. 5", $100.00; 7", $150.00; 9", $175.00.

Ohio Star Square Plate (Small)

Here is the 6" square plate from which the 5¼" mint dish shown elsewhere was made. The plate, of course, is much rarer and only a handful of these are reported. It was made in 1910 but to the best of our knowledge wasn't advertised as the mint dish was. 6", $250.00.

Ohio Star Large Square Plate

This large size square plate has an entirely different look from the small square plate shown elsewhere and doesn't have the center star. This large example was flattened from the large ice cream bowl shape with only the four points turned slightly up. $500.00.

Ohio Star Stemmed Rose Bowl Whimsey

Made from the 4½" compote mould, this little cutie has been turned in very tightly so that only an opening about the size of a half-dollar exists at the top. The whole appearance is that of a very finely carved ball on a stem and it is one of the best of all the whimsies in Millersburg crystal. The glass is polished and sparkles with a special glow. I must confess, this piece and the cider pitcher are my favorite shapes in Ohio Star. We've seen this rose bowl whimsey with the top less closed also. $300.00.

Ohio Star Syrup Jug

Over the years, I've heard about nine of these little jugs and none of the owners seem willing to ever part with theirs. They stand 5¼" tall and are quite hefty for their size. Often the metal tops have damage but that doesn't seem to bring down their desirability in the least. The handle is notched, just like those on the toothpick holder, and we're relatively sure these weren't given away at the factory or there would be more of them around. $600.00, rare.

Ohio Star Butter Dish

Hard to find, seldom seen without damage on the inner rim of the base, and massively designed, this covered butter dish is a treasure. The glass is heavy and sparkling and the patterning perfect, even to the starred knob. $250.00.

Ohio Star Creamer

With a squat shape and deeply incised design, this creamer is a beauty. It has a notched handle like the spooner and covered sugar. Millersburg advertised this pattern as a "polished" glass and it is just that. $150.00.

Ohio Star Spooner

The two-handled spooner in this pattern is squat and ovid in shape. The glass is thick, giving the piece a heavy look, and the design is deep and bold, but the spooner looks a bit small when standing beside the covered sugar. $150.00.

Ohio Star Covered Sugar

A heavy match for the covered butter dish, this piece is very impressive indeed. It sparkles and the deep design fills every bit of available space, even to the top of the finial where the Ohio Star is repeated. $200.00.

Ohio Star Tankard Pitcher

Sometimes called the Ohio Star variant pitcher, this one is 9½" tall and is very rare. We've now heard of five of these (the first I'd seen was in 1980 in the Covert collection) and believe me, everyone would like to own one! Please note the handle is applied like the Hobstar and Feather Mammoth pitcher. $1,500.00, very rare.

Ohio Star Toothpick Holder

Here is that famous piece that supposedly started Millersburg collecting. This article was given away that first week the company was in operation. The toothpick holder is 2½" tall and 4" across from handle to handle. The handles are notched just like those on the syrups and the glass is usually very good quality (I have seen a couple that were dull and grayish). Nonetheless, this little piece is one most Millersburg collectors wouldn't do without and it is always a good place to start a new collection, even if the prices are rather steep. $125.00.

Ohio Star Small Tri-Cornered Bowl

Seldom seen or sold, this beautiful whimsey bowl is shaped from the sauce or ice cream bowl. It measures about 5½" in diameter at the widest point. Interestingly enough, this piece is also found in a rare marigold carnival item as well as an even rarer white carnival piece, so someone must have liked this whimsey shape at the factory. Some collectors call this a clover-leaf shape also. $150.00.

Ohio Star Large Tri-Cornered Bowl

Pulled form the large ice cream bowl, this one has been turned up on three sides and left nearly flat on another to give it this strange tri-cornered look. It measures 10" x 11" and has five stars around the sides. $250.00. We're grateful to Wally McDaniel for sharing this rare item with us.

Ohio Star Standard Pitcher

This pitcher is found less often than the cider pitcher but not as seldom as the tankard. This one has a flowing bell shaping with the lip greatly flared and an applied handle. It is about 2" shorter than the cider pitcher. $450.00.

Ohio Star Tumblers (Standard and Cider)

We are happy to show these two Ohio Star tumblers together so beginners can see just how different they are. The belled cider tumbler is on the left and is slightly taller than the standard tumbler on the right which does not bell. The standard tumblers are much scarcer than the cider ones and usually sell for more. Cider, $55.00; standard, $100.00.

Ohio Star Vase

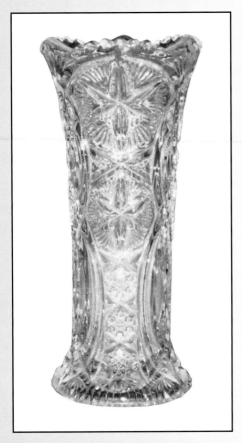

Probably one of the most recognized pieces of Millersburg crystal, this 10" tall vase is a standout. The glass is thick and sparkling, with a gentle flair from the middle up to the top and down to the base. Besides the normal ones, we've seen two whimsey shapes in this vase. One was a tri-cornered top with the three lips turned down, and the second was a jack-in-the-pulpit whimsey that rested in a large Millersburg window display at the Festival in 1999. Both are very rare and may well be one-of-a-kind novelties. Of course the vase is also found in carnival glass in amethyst, green, marigold, and clambroth. $375.00.

Ohio Star Vase Whimsey

We've seen two versions of a whimsey in this vase; a JIP shape, and the tri-cornered one shown here. To date, we've heard of three or four of these and a couple of the JIP, but all are very desirable and a real find for collection. $1,500.00 – 1,700.00.

Cherry Jardiniere Whimsey

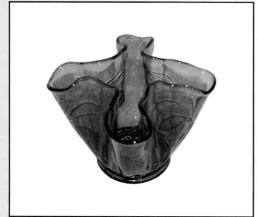

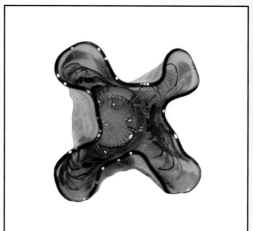

What a rare and beautiful item this whimsey is. It is in emerald green crystal and was shaped from a large bowl or plate with the sides being turned up and then ruffled, leaving the cherry design on the inside and the exterior plain. It is the only reported example. $2,000.00 – 3,000.00. Thanks to Ben Hershberger for this rariety.

Swirl Hobnail and Tulip Colonial Pieces

Although well known in carnival glass, neither of these patterns is often thought of in crystal, but here they are. The spittoon shape in the Swirl Hobnail pattern is the only non-iridized example we've heard about and it is on amethyst glass. (Where's the crystal one?)

The Tulip compote is found with either the Rosalind or the Flowering Vine interiors in carnival, but can also be found iridized without an interior design. Here it is in crystal and it is distinguished by the eight-sided base and the small panels down the stem. It is very graceful and stands about 8" – 9" tall. Top shapings include the deep bowl with a flared rim, a deep ruffled rim, or the flared and ruffled salver shape shown. All shapes in both carnival glass or crystal are rare and desirable.

Swirl Hobnail Spittoon (Amethyst)

What a rare beauty this is! For years I've dreamed of finding one in crystal. This example is on amethyst glass but without any carnival treatment. It is a very desirable Millersburg item indeed. $2,500.00, very rare. Courtesy of Steve Maag.

Tulip Deep Compote

If you've ever examined the three or four known Tulip compotes in carnival glass, you will see this is exactly the same shape with a deep bowl and six ruffles. It was also the same compote mould that was used to produce the tall Rosalind or the Flowering Vine compote with added interior plungers. The crystal pieces are all very rare and are known in at least three shapes. One is a ruffled compote and the other is a very shallow ruffled card stand shown elsewhere. When I found this shape in a Burlington, Kentucky, shop, the owner told me it had been one of a set of six, all shaped exactly alike, so we can estimate about a dozen compotes in all shapes are known. $500.00.

Tulip Goblet

Just like the compote and the salver shapes shown elsewhere, here is the goblet shape in the Tulip compote (Flowering Vine or tall Rosalind blanks). All shapes are rare and desirable but this one probably leads the list of hardest to find. $650.00.

Pulled or shaped from the regular deep shape, this piece has been flattened and then ruffled, giving it a tray shaping. It stands 7½" tall and has a bowl diameter of about 8½". The stem is paneled as is the octagon-shaped base. We've heard of six of these rarities and I am very thrilled to have one in my collection. These were part of the Millersburg Flute line and the glass is about as clear and sparkling as it gets. $650.00.

Millersburg Water Sets in Crystal

While there are several outstanding water sets from the Millersburg factory in carnival glass, only the Cherry, Diamonds, Marilyn, and Feather and Heart patterns are known without iridescence. (This of course does not include the Ohio Star and Hobstar and Feather pieces that were the backbone of Millersburg's crystal production.)

Can you just imagine what excitement a crystal Multifruits and Flowers or a Morning Glory crystal water set would cause? We feel the reason these patterns were excluded is they were more decorative than utilitarian.

At any rate, we are happy to show the Feather and Heart pitcher and tumbler here as well as the Marilyn pitcher (no tumblers are currently known). Each is a heavy, geometric masterpiece with clear glass and deep design. In addition we show elsewhere the Diamonds tumbler in amethyst crystal and have heard there exists a crystal pitcher and a tumbler in this pattern as well as a Diamonds punch bowl base and a base whimsey that has been pulled into an oval compote shape when up-ended.

Cherry

We've learned of two of these water pitchers (there is also one known milk pitcher) in crystal. They are from the same moulds as the carnival examples but so much rarer, and it is a real privilege to show one here. Water pitcher, $1,200.00; milk pitcher, $1,000.00. Thanks to Jerry Hall for sharing this beauty.

Marilyn

First advertised in Butler Brothers catalog in the winter of 1909, this pitcher is better known in carnival glass, but can be found rarely in crystal. Unlike the carnival set, no tumblers have been reported in crystal, but perhaps one will eventually turn up. This pitcher and the Feather and Heart pitcher were advertised alone (without tumblers) but the latter has proved to have matching crystal tumblers. At any rate, the Marilyn crystal pitcher is a rare item and is always in demand by collectors. $525.00.

Feather and Heart Pitcher

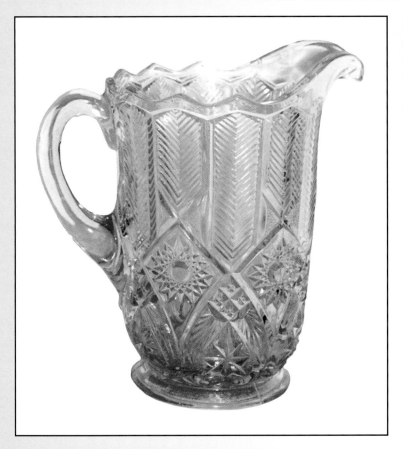

Not quite as rare as the matching tumblers shown elsewhere, this pitcher is one of the real finds nonetheless. It is just like the carnival version but in crystal and is shown in 1911 Butler Brothers ads from Millersburg. $450.00.

Feather and Heart Tumbler

Just why more of these tumblers that match the water pitcher weren't made is a mystery. To say they are rare in crystal is an understatement. Here is one of the handful reported (we honestly believe that less than a dozen exist in all collections) and it is a privilege to show them. The water pitcher was advertised in crystal without matching tumblers so it may be that these known are just leftovers that were not given a marigold iridizing when carnival water sets were made. $75.00 each.

Diamonds Punch Base

We once saw this base for the punch set pulled out into a compote shape, but here it is just as it was meant to be used. Surely the bowl is out there somewhere, and to unite them would be a real joy. Punch bowl, $525.00, rare; base, $225.00, rare.

Diamonds Tumbler

We are happy to show one of the Diamonds tumblers in amethyst glass that wasn't iridized. Besides the tumbler we've heard there is also an amethyst uniridized pitcher as well as crystal examples of each. $375.00, rare.

The Guessing Game

Now we come to the question marks, all excellent patterns that have a clarity of glass and a sparkle that seems to shout Millersburg, but just can't be pinned down at this time.

We know, for example, the Honeycomb and Hobstar vase was made in carnival glass at Millersburg, period. But what about the crystal vase, or the other shapes in this pattern that include a water set, berry set, table set, toothpick holder, vases, and a compote? We know these were first Ohio Flint Glass Company patterns, sold when that plant closed in 1907, to Jefferson Glass, who in turn sold the moulds (or at least some of them) to Millersburg. Ohio Flint called this pattern Gloria.

Or the Venetian pattern which began life as Kenneth, another Ohio Flint pattern that traveled the same route. We know that Millersburg made the giant rose bowl and the table set in carnival. What about the other shapes and what about crystal pieces?

And then there is Riverside's Lucille oil lamp line. We know John Fenton bought these moulds when Riverside closed but did he make any or all of these lamps in crystal?

Finally, we have a variant Flute pattern we strongly suspect was made at Millersburg and is called "river glass" by many of today's collectors, who say it was called that by their parents and was made in eastern Ohio and shipped down the river.

Perhaps we will never really know the full history of these patterns but we are happy to show samples of them here and open up the discussion for your consideration. Certainly each in its own way has some link with the Millersburg plant (or seems to) and it would be a shame to eliminate them without further investigation.

1907 ad showing Riverside's Lucille line of lamps. Note the example on the right later became the basis for Millersburg's Wild Rose Colonial, and Ladies' Medallion lamps.

Colonial Hand Lamp

If you will compare this lamp with the Wild Rose hand lamp shown elsewhere, you will see they are virtually the same, but the Colonial has no floral design. Whether John Fenton just removed these flowers and leaves from the mould or this was actually a separate design, we can't say, but we feel both lamps were eventually made at Millersburg. Only in recent years have we even known of these hand lamps and both of them add a new dimension to the Millersburg picture. As you can see, this lamp has no "Riverside Clinch-on Collar" lettering as does the other lamp. Base is 5¾" diameter. $500.00, rare.

Ladies' Medallion Lamp

On June 6, 1906, the Riverside Glass company advertised this lamp in their Lucille lamp line in *China, Glass & Lamps*. The lamp honored the Riverside Glass Company's owners' wives. A year later, the Riverside plant closed and John Fenton owned this lamp mould as well as the Riverside Wild Rose lamps and the Colonial lamps (all a part of the Lucille group). When Mr. Fenton opened the Millersburg Glass Company, he produced these lamps in carnival, and possibly crystal, removing the Riverside Clinch-on Collar lettering on some but not on all of these lamps. $1,200.00, rare.

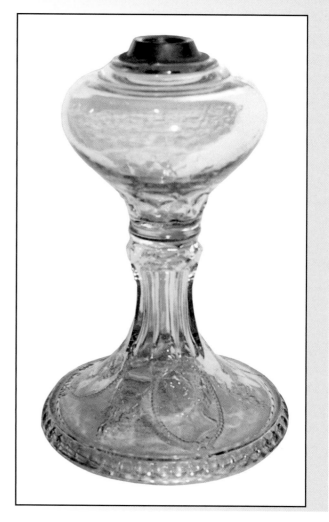

Wild Rose Hand Lamp

This is just like the Colonial Hand Lamp shown elsewhere except for the roses and leaves design (this is has the "Riverside Clinch-on Collar" lettering). This lamp in this size and shape wasn't reported until recently (we first saw it at the Millersburg Festival in 1999). In design it is exactly like the other Wild Rose lamps, but smaller, and we can now say there are at least four sizes in this lamp design. All these lamps were part of Riverside's Lucille line that also included the Ladies' Medallion line and were purchased by John Fenton after Riverside closed in 1907. Table lamp, $500.00; hand lamp, $650.00, rare.

Venetian and Honeycomb & Hobstar

As we've said both of these patterns originated at the Ohio Flint Glass plant that closed in 1907. The moulds were then sold to Jefferson Glass, and John Fenton purchased some of them when he began the Millersburg operation.

Venetian (Kenneth) was a large line at Ohio Flint and shapes included a table set, water set, berry set, squat water pitcher, punch set, hotel creamer and sugar, milk pitcher, pickle dish, celery boat, oil bottle, water bottle, vases in at least two sizes, a large rose bowl that can be found made into a spittoon whimsey or a compote, and a medium size stemmed compote that can also be found whimsied into a rose bowl. Perhaps there are other shapes we haven't seen yet.

The Honeycomb and Hobstar (Gloria) pattern is found in a table set, water set, berry set, oil bottle, water bottle, and perhaps other shapes as well. It is well known in ruby stain and with gilding too.

It is nearly impossible to state with any accuracy where the Ohio Flint pieces begin in crystal and where Millersburg may have taken over. We do know these patterns were probably not made by Jefferson Glass at all. But since both the Venetian giant rose bowl and the table set are known in carnival glass and the Honeycomb and Hobstar vase is also found iridized, Millersburg did produce both patterns. Only years of future research may shed more light on these patterns, but we strongly suspect Millersburg did produce some crystal pieces in both patterns.

123

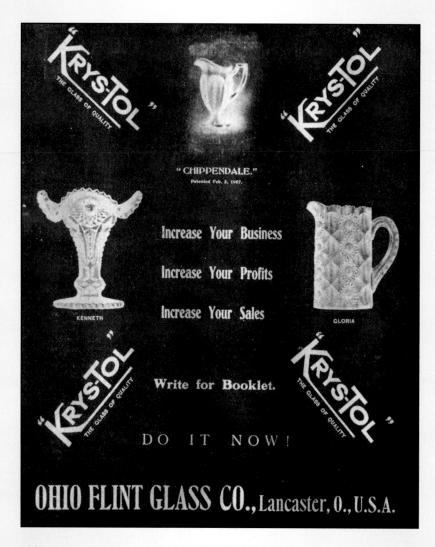

1907 Ohio Flint Glass ad showing their Chippendale line as well as the Gloria (Honeycomb & Hobstar) and Kenneth (Venetian) patterns that were later made at Millersburg.

Butler Brothers catalog ad for the Venetian punch set in crystal. The ad ran in October 1909, the first edition to show ads from Millersburg, nearly two years after Ohio Flint Glass had closed.

Cambridge #2340 oil lamp, composed of their large bowl in the #2631 Marjorie or Sweetheart pattern paired with Millersburg's Venetian (Kenneth) rose bowl, purchased when the Millersburg factory closed.

Honeycomb and Hobstar Compote

As we said earlier, this pattern was originally called Gloria and was made by the Ohio Flint Glass Company in 1906. In 1907 Ohio Flint closed, the moulds for this pattern were sold to Jefferson Glass, and in 1909 John Fenton bought at least some of them to use (at least the vase mould). Here we are happy to show the scarce compote shape that is 5" tall and has a top diameter of 6". It is very clear and sparkling glass, much like what we've come to expect from the Millersburg Company but we have no proof it was ever made there even though this piece is unmarked. $150.00.

Honeycomb and Hobstar Flared Compote

Like the regular compote shown elsewhere in this pattern, this example is flared greatly. It measures 5" tall and 9" across the top. As we've said, we have no proof this piece was ever made at Millersburg but the possibility can't be dismissed without more knowledge. $150.00.

Honeycomb and Hobstar Covered Butter Dish

We have no knowledge that this shape was made at the Millersburg factory but we're showing it just in case. $150.00.

Honeycomb and Hobstar Vase (Flared)

Here is a flared version of this rare vase to compare with the squared top version we show elsewhere. Both are about equal in rarity but for some reason, I like this flared one better than the other shape. $500.00.

Honeycomb and Hobstar Square-Top Vase

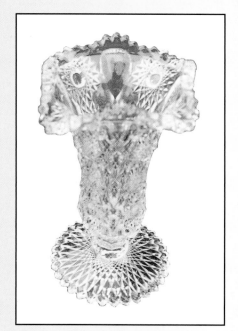

Besides the flared, tri-cornered, and rose bowl shaped tops on this vase, the most often seen is the square-topped ones. We've heard of about six or seven in this shaping and while they are very nice, they do not show off the design as well as the flared example. $500.00.

Honeycomb and Hobstar Vase

Here is the vase John Fenton made in carnival glass from the original Ohio Flint Glass mould. We can't begin to confirm just how many of the moulds John Fenton purchased when Ohio Flint closed, but this one we can, and we honestly believe some of these crystal vases are Millersburg. The top can be flared, square, or widely squared like the example shown. $500.00.

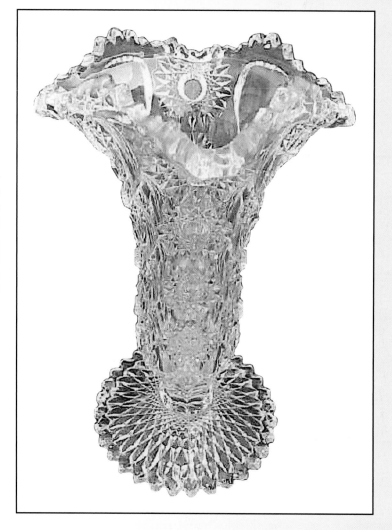

Honeycomb and Hobstar Vase (Rose Bowl Top Shape)

Besides the flared top and the tri-cornered top (both shown elsewhere), this vase can be found with four corners turned down (called a square top), and this very rare rose bowl shaped top. It only proves just how inventive glassmakers were, trying to get as much mileage out of a single mould as possible. $500.00.

Venetian Giant Compote Whimsey

Here is a third shape pulled from the giant rose bowl mould and it isn't often seen. It measures 6½" tall and has a bowl diameter of 10", having been pulled out and flattened to an ice cream shape, just like the Hobstar and Feather whimsey (another hint they were made by the same shapers). This is a rare shape for this pattern and we've encountered only the one example. $250.00.

Venetian Giant Rose Bowl

From the same mould as the carnival examples, the crystal pieces have serrated rims. They stand about 10" tall and are very heavy, just like the Hobstar and Feather giant rose bowls. The bases and stems are nearly identical too. As we said earlier, this mould was first made at Ohio Flint Glass as the Kenneth line but when the company closed, the moulds came to Jefferson Glass who sold them to Millersburg. We cannot say just who made which item, but we feel certain Millersburg made some of the crystal pieces so we are showing an assortment of them here for collectors to see. $150.00.

Venetian Giant Spittoon Whimsey

From the same mould as the giant rose bowl and the ice cream stand, this beautiful piece has the edges turned out in a shape that looks square from the top and is a quite attractive shaping. It is nearly as tall as the rose bowl (10") and would certainly grace any collection of fine crystal. The design is flawless and the centers of the hobstars are prismatic. $150.00.

Venetian Master Berry Bowl

Talk about thick glass! This piece measures 9" across, is 4½" deep, and has a glass thickness of more than ½"! We're sure there were small berry bowls to match this piece and sets were probably made in ruffled shapes too, but we've only seen the one bowl to date. The design continues all the way under the bowl, which isn't ground but sits on the four diamonds of the design itself — a very well planned happening. $50.00.

Venetian Medium Compote

Here is the piece seen in the Ohio Flint ads (along with a vase shape from the same mould). It has an 8" top diameter and stands 6" tall. The odd thing about this piece is that the foot is plain (unlike the rest of the Venetian footed pieces that all have serrated edges and a base hobstar), and it has eight sides. It is marked "krys-tol." $150.00.

Venetian Medium Stemmed Rose Bowl

Pulled from the same mould as the medium compote shape, this stunning rose bowl has the top turned in greatly and is a real show stopper. Norm Archer owns this piece and I sure wish I had one. $200.00.

Venetian Milk Pitcher

Shaped like the hotel pieces and the squat pitcher, this milk pitcher is 6½" tall. Like all Venetian pieces the center of the hobstar has a prismatic button just like some Millersburg Hobstar and Feather pieces. $50.00.

Venetian Motel Creamer

Unlike the standard table set pieces, this creamer is taller, and generally has a shape that matches the squat pitcher, as well as the milk pitcher. This piece is unmarked. $50.00.

Venetian Oil Bottle

We've now seen two of these and both had flaws (this one leans and the other was cracked). This oil cruet stands 6½" tall and is on thinner glass. The base has a pontil indicating it is mould blown. We believe the stopper is original since it matches the finials on the table set pieces. $35.00.

Venetian Pickle Dish (Small)

We believe there must be more than one size of these pickle dishes and the example shown here measures 7½" long and 4¼" wide. The glass is very thick and we can guess that this mould may have yielded bowls as well as the pickle dish. It is marked "krys-tol." $35.00.

Venetian Celery Boat

This deep, boat-shaped celery holder is 10½" long and is shaped exactly like the pickle dish shown above. The glass is thick and very clear and the design flawless. $85.00.

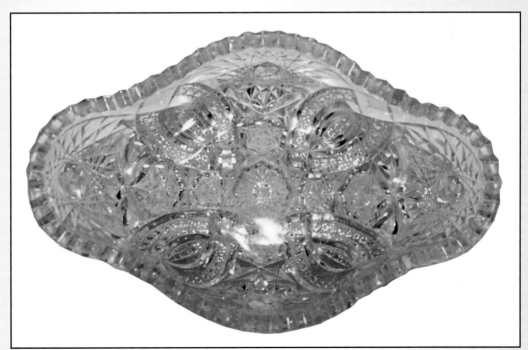

Venetian Punch Set

Shown in an October 1909 ad (Ohio Flint closed in late 1907), that also features the first Millersburg ads, this outstanding punch set is about as beautiful as glass gets. The base is extremely decorative as is the bowl, and the cups are on a stem with the same base design and a squared handle, just like the squat pitcher we show elsewhere. Each piece is marked "krys-tol" but we've only seen the one bowl and base and one

cup, so this must be a rather scarce set. Bowl and base, $500.00, rare; stemmed cup, $25.00 each.

Venetian Small Compote Whimsey

Shaped from the 6½" rose bowl shown elsewhere, this piece has been opened out into a compote shape. Notice that the serrated top has been smoothed into ovals, unlike the other shapes. This compote is 5¼" tall and has a top diameter of 6". $75.00.

Venetian Small Rose Bowl

Shaped pretty much like the larger version, this 6½"
stemmed piece has the top turned in and there are four
rings below, with a series of oval dimples just above the
rings. We know of three shapes from this mould (we show
all three) but there may be others. $75.00.

Venetian Small Spittoon Whimsey

Pulled from the same 6½" stemmed rose bowl shape, this one has
the top flared like a spittoon. Please note there are rings below the
top on this size and there are also dimples just under the rim. The
stem and foot are just like the larger versions of this pattern.
$75.00.

Venetian Squat Pitcher

Standing 6" tall and with a 7" top diameter, this very heavy squat pitcher is a real find and the first one we've seen. The glass is top quality and unlike most pieces of Venetian, this one doesn't have the "krys-tol" or "crys-tal" marking. The base contains a huge hobstar with a prismatic center, matching the rest of the design. $95.00.

Venetian Covered Butter Dish

Just like the rare carnival examples, this butter dish is well designed from its tall finial to the well patterned base. The glass is thick and clear and the pieces are very scarce. $100.00.

Venetian Standard Creamer

Here is the creamer that has been found iridized so we can assume Millersburg had some production of this shape at its factory. It is a low, graceful piece and the entire table set is a real show stopper. $45.00.

Venetian Standard Covered Sugar

Here is the standard or table set covered sugar. It is the one that has been found iridized at the Millersburg factory so we know this piece, like the matching butter dish, creamer, and spooner were made at Millersburg. $60.00.

Venetian Tankard Water Pitcher

This heavy, massive pitcher stands 9½" tall and has the same shaped handle and pouring spout as the Hobstar and Feather pitcher. It also has a pontil or sheer mark on the base. The glass is clear and quite thick and the pitcher doesn't have the "Krys-tol" mark. We now know of three of these pitchers in collections in the Midwest. $150.00.

Venetian Water Bottle

Slightly larger than the Ohio Star water bottle in width, the Venetian one is just as heavy and just as deeply moulded. It has a pontil mark on the base and the glass is clear and sparkling. $150.00. Courtesy of the Westons.

Venetian Stemmed Vase (Small)

Here is the 10" stemmed vase shown in the ad at the beginning of this section that Ohio Flint Glass featured. It is turned out into a broad squared top, making it shorter than the flared examples. In addition, there is a 14" vase and possibly a 12" one too. Top shapings of these vases include flared, ruffled, squared, and rose bowl shaped. $100.00.

"River Glass"

For the past few years, we've encountered pieces of this Flute or Wide Panel variation that was shown in a winter 1910 edition of the Butler Brothers catalog (they called it their Santa Claus Edition). When we examined the bowls, we found the marie design and the fluting matched some Millersburg carnival bowls, namely the Millersburg Grape bowls and one without an interior pattern. For this reason we are showing a sampling of the bowls but the ad also included a water pitcher, syrup jug, oil cruet, a two-handled celery vase, and table set.

The ad called this a "world beater" colonial assortment, full finished with star bottoms. It sold for 86 cents a dozen. The bowls are shown in three sizes (we've actually seen four sizes), and were ruffled, round, or flared. The glass of all pieces we've seen is clear and sparkling, matching Millersburg glass in every way and the carnival pieces have a radium finish.

We certainly can't verify the stories about this glass coming down the river but it does seem odd that we heard it from more than one source in the shops. Only time and more information will tell us if this is truly Millersburg, but we feel it needed to be explored and exposed for collectors to ponder.

1910 Butler Brothers ad showing a selection of Flute or Wide Panel pieces that are commonly called "river glass" by Ohio collectors. We believe these are Millersburg pieces since the bowl is the same exterior as the carnival Millersburg Grape piece.

River Glass Flute Bowl

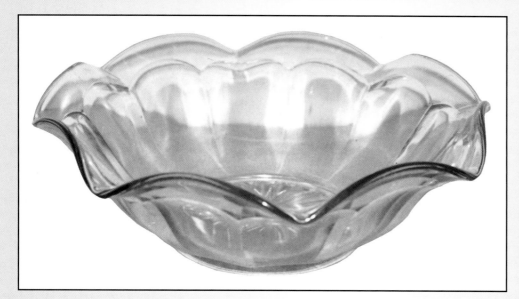

We've heard of these bowls in 5", 7", 8", and 9" sizes, and the 1910 Butler Brothers ad shows them with a six-ruffled top, a flared round top, or a round straight top. The base is 20-rayed on the 9" bowl, and 18-rayed on the 8" bowl. The rays are exactly like those on the Millersburg Grape bowl in carnival glass, as are the exterior flutes (these are 12 in number). The glass is extremely clear and sparkling. Bowl, $25.00 – 35.00 each.

Bibliography

Edwards, Bill. *Millersburg Crystal Glassware*. Paducah, KY: Collector Books, 1982.

Edwards, Bill and Mike Carwile. *Standard Encyclopedia of Carnival Glass, 7th edition*. Paducah, KY: Collector Books, 2000.

—. *Standard Encyclopedia of Opalescent Glass, 3rd edition*. Paducah, KY: Collector Books, 1999.

—. *Standard Encyclopedia of Pressed Glass, 2nd edition*. Paducah, KY: Collector Books, 2000.

Gorham, C.W. *Riverside Glass Works*. Springfield, MO: Highlights, 1995.

Kamm, Minnie Watson. *Pattern Glass Pitchers I – VIII*. Self-published, 1943.

McGee, Marie. *Millersburg Glass*. Marietta, Ohio: The Glass Press, Inc., 1995.

Welker, Mary, Lyle, and Lynn. *The Cambridge Glass Co., vol. I, II*. Newark, Ohio, self-published, 1974.

About the Authors

Bill Edwards is a native Hoosier, Navy veteran, retired banker, and a writer of glass books for Collector Books. He wrote the first book about Millersburg glass in 1972 and has been author or co-author of 19 other glass books since then. He lives in Madison, Indiana.

Mike Carwile was born in 1953 in Brookneal, Virginia, where he grew up in a family of antique collectors. His interest covered a general line of collecting until the 1980s when he began to specialize in antique glass. In the early to mid 1990s, he joined up with Bill Edwards and has co-authored the following books: *The Standard Encyclopedia of Carnival Glass, 6th Edition; The Standard Encyclopedia of Carnival Glass, 7th Edition; The Standard Encyclopedia of Pressed Glass, 1st Edition; The Standard Encyclopedia of Pressed Glass, 2nd Editon; The Standard Encyclopedia of Millersburg Crystal;* and *The Standard Encyclopedia of Opalescent Glass, 3rd Edition.*

He now lives in Lynchburg, Virginia, along with his wife Janet, son Evan, and daughter Jillian Grant.